MALCOLM McDONALD ON MARKETING PLANNING

UNDERSTANDING MARKETING PLANS AND STRATEGY

KoganPage

LONDON   PHILADELPHIA   NEW DELHI

First published in Great Britain in 2002 by Kogan Page Limited entitled *If You're So Brilliant...
How Come Your Marketing Plans Aren't Working?*

Reissued in 2008 entitled *Malcolm McDonald on Marketing Planning*
Reprinted 2008, 2012

120 Pentonville Road	1518 Walnut Street, Suite 1100	4737/23 Ansari Road
London N1 9JN	Philadelphia PA 19102	Danyaganj
United Kingdom	USA	New Delhi 110002
www.koganpage.com		India

© Malcolm McDonald, 2002, 2005, 2008

ISBN 978 0 7494 5149 3

British Library Cataloguing in Publication Data

A CIP record for this book is available from the British Library.

Library of Congress Cataloging-in-Publication Data

McDonald, Malcolm
  [How come your marketing plans aren't working?]
  Malcolm McDonald on marketing planning : understanding marketing plans
and strategy / Malcolm McDonald
      p. cm.
  Includes index.
  ISBN 978-0-7494-5149-3
1 Marketing–Planning. 2. Marketing–Management. I. McDonald,
Malcolm. How come your marketing plans aren't working? II. Title.
  HF5415.13 M369157 2007
  658.8902--dc22
                          2007037090

Typeset by Saxon Graphics Ltd, Derby
Print production managed by Jellyfish
Printed and bound by CPI Group (UK) Ltd, Croydon, CR0 4YY

MALCOLM McDONALD ON MARKETING PLANNING

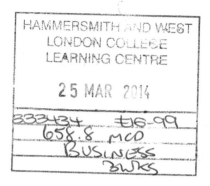

Contents

Important note from the author

This is a text for busy managers who don't have time to wade through voluminous texts. Accordingly, its strengths are that it contains only the essentials necessary for marketing planning. Its weaknesses are that it gives only brief treatment to some of the really complex issues that get in the way of effective marketing planning, such as corporate culture, politics, organizational structures, knowledge, skills and a host of other items. Nonetheless, the essentials are here and those who want and need a quick and effective guide will find it in this useful little book.

It covers the essentials of marketing planning and contains a number of test questions at the end of each chapter. Whilst these are by no means essential to the learning process, they do nonetheless provide a quick check on understanding. Of much more significance are the two 'tests' in Chapter 1. Please ensure you complete these.

For those who need a totally professional approach to strategic and tactical marketing planning, I refer you to my main text on this subject: *Marketing Plans: How to prepare them; how to use them* (Butterworth-Heinemann, Oxford, 2007, 6th edition). Much of the thinking and some of the exercises and diagrams have been borrowed from this widely used and respected global text.

Finally, this book would not have been possible without the editorial assistance of Margrit Bass of Native Arrows (native.arrows@tiscali.co.uk). Her perceptive insights and writing skills are second to none.

Preface

In the present business climate of increasingly competitive markets, there is a growing realization that success in the future will come only from meticulous planning and market preparation. In order to make a confident commitment to the future, an organization's marketing plans must be meaningful: they must be relevant, realistic, and useable. To be of any benefit, marketing plans must accurately portray the known corporate and market environments as well as provide an educated guide through unknown terrain, given the inevitability of change.

There are three distinct yet interdependent stages involved in developing strategic marketing capability in an organization:

- Establish a disciplined framework, or logic, for undertaking the marketing planning process and producing strategies.
- Underpin this framework with a meaningful marketing intelligence function (which may or may not reside within a specific department)
- Undertake the necessary steps inside the organization to convert the written plans into actionable propositions. These steps will likely involve change in organizational culture, structure and operations, which is best driven by the leadership and commitment of the CEO.

A working marketing plan *is* achievable, providing you are equipped with a sound understanding of the aims and principles of marketing planning, and are prepared to make the right investment in terms of time, energy, resources and commitment. This book sets out to impart such understanding through concise explanation of the key concepts and instruction in undertaking the requisite planning steps. Readers are invited to test their knowledge and progress by completing the Question and Answer sections at the close of each chapter, and the educational tests included in some chapters.

Introduction

After 50 years of marketing, developing a marketing strategy that is sufficiently robust to guide the rest of the organization about how it can build superior value for its customers remains one of the most elusive of all marketing skills.

Research into marketing planning carried out at Cranfield during 25 years reveals a truly appalling level of competence in this central function of marketing. Indeed, things seem to be getting worse rather than better, and over 10 years since the famous Brady and Davis criticism of the whole marketing domain, marketing people are still seen as 'expensive, slippery and unaccountable'.

Our research also shows an unacceptably low level of competence in basic marketing skills. Many so-called 'practitioners' have not even heard of most of the diagnostic tools of the trade necessary for

Levels of competence in marketing are still very low

producing a good, solid marketing plan, and the percentage of qualified marketers (in the sense of having passed the appropriate marketing examinations) is at an all-time low. What, we wonder, would happen to a would-be accountant, architect, banker, or engineer who thought they could get a job without passing appropriate standards? Even more depressing, marketing practitioners have this awful habit of blaming everyone else in the organization for their own failure to have much impact on the espoused strategy.

So, with such a blatant and devastatingly honest and up-front commentary on the state of marketing, what is this book about? Excellent marketing planning is a core requirement for marketers and this little book tackles this topic head on. It takes all the mystery out of it and acts as a straightforward 'this is how you do it' guide to this most difficult but essential of marketing processes.

Marketing planning is a core requirement for marketers

First, however, let's get a fix on how well your company seems to be performing generally. The following Introductory Test is not a trick questionnaire, but if you don't score very well, it will certainly confirm that you need help. If you score brilliantly well, I recommend that you quickly move on to the core section of this book, which begins with Chapter 3.

Introductory Test:
Evaluation of organizational performance*

Place a tick after each statement in the column that most accurately describes your organization's situation.

	Very true	True	Don't know	Untrue	Very untrue
1 (a) Our return on invested capital is satisfactory.					
(b) There is good evidence it will stay that way for the next five years.					
(c) Detailed analysis indicates that it is probably incapable of being materially improved.					
2 (a) Our market share is not declining.					
(b) This is a fact, based on objective evidence.					
(c) There is objective evidence that it will stay that way.					
3 (a) Our turnover is increasing.					
(b) At a rate faster than inflation.					
(c) But not at the expense of profitability.					
4 I know for sure that our sales organization is only allowed to push less profitable lines at the expense of more profitable ones if there are rational reasons for doing so.					

*This test is adapted from *Marketing Plans: How to prepare them; how to use them*, Malcolm McDonald, Butterworth-Heinemann, Oxford, 6th edition, 2007.

	Very true	True	Don't know	Untrue	Very untrue
5 (a) I understand why the company has performed the way it has during the past five years.					
(b) I know (apart from hoping) where it is heading during the next five years.					
6 (a) I am wholly satisfied that we make what the market wants, not what we prefer to produce.					
(b) Our operations, R&D, IT, HR, finance, marketing and selling strategies are developed for the profitability of the company as a whole rather than for the gratification of any personal ambitions.					
(c) I am satisfied that we do not use short-term tactics which are injurious to our long-term interests.					
7 (a) I know that sales and profit forecasts presented by operating management are realistic.					
(b) I know they are as exacting as they can reasonably be.					
(c) If I or anyone insists that they are raised, it is because a higher level is attainable not just because a better-looking budget is required.					
8 (a) The detailed data generated internally are analysed to provide timely information about what is happening in the key areas of the business.					

	Very true	True	Don't know	Untrue	Very untrue
(b) Marketing research data which operating management acquires is synthesized into plain English, and is actually needed and used in the key decision-making process.					
9 (a) We do not sell unprofitably to any customer.					
(b) We analyse our figures to be sure of this.					
(c) If we do, it is for rational reasons known to us all.					
10 Our marketing policies are based on market-centred opportunities which we have fully researched, not on vague hopes of doing better.					

Join up the ticks down the page and count how many are to the left of the **don't know** position, and how many are at the *don't know* position or to the right of it.

Interpretation of Introductory Test
If you have 11 or more answers in the *don't know* position or to the right of it, then the chances are that your company isn't very market-driven. It needs to take a closer look at itself. But are you sure? If not, you're going to have to work really hard at marketing.

Scores between 12 and 20 to the left of the *don't know* position indicate an organization that appears to have a reasonable control of many of the significant ingredients of commercial success. Nonetheless, there is clearly still room for improvement.

Scores above 20 to the left of the *don't know* position indicate an organization completely in command of the key success variables. Are you certain that this is a true reflection of your organization's situation? If you are, then the chances are that its marketing skills are already highly developed and that you are probably already doing a reasonably good marketing job.

Understanding marketing planning

Widespread ignorance about marketing planning and confusion about the difference between strategic marketing planning, and sales forecasting and budgeting, has caused many an organization to strive short of its full potential or, indeed, to die prematurely without the real root cause of death ever being identified. Such agonizing outcomes can be avoided to a great extent by fully understanding what marketing planning is (and is not), and assimilating this understanding in actual practice.

To acquire an understanding of marketing planning, it is necessary first to gain an appreciation of the role of marketing within the business context. When Adam Smith said back in 1776 that consumption is the sole end and purpose of production, he was in fact describing what has been termed the marketing concept. Central to the marketing concept is the idea that marketing is a matching process between a company's capabilities and the wants and needs of customers in order to achieve the objectives of both parties. Marketing is thus about providing goods and services for which there is a known customer demand, rather than selling what the company likes to produce.

The purpose of *marketing planning* and its principal focus are the identification and creation of competitive advantage. Marketing planning is the planned application of marketing resources to achieve marketing objectives. Given the increasing turbulence and complexity of the marketplace, and the rapid pace of technological change, the need for a disciplined, systematic approach to the market has never been so acute. The most marked difference in marketing planning today, as compared to yesteryear, is that all levels of management are involved, with the resulting intelligence coming from the market rather than from the heads of a remote group of planners with little or no operational involvement.

> The purpose of marketing planning is the identification and creation of competitive advantage

The current trend in successful businesses is towards an emphasis on scanning the external environment, identifying early the forces emanating from it, and developing appropriate strategic responses. *Strategic marketing planning* is a management process leading to a marketing plan. It is a logical sequence and a series of activities leading to the setting of marketing objectives and formulation of plans for achieving them. (The precise steps in this process and the contents of a marketing plan are the subject of Chapter 3.) In small, undiversified companies this process is usually informal whereas in larger, more diversified organizations, the process is often systematized.

THE NEED FOR A SYSTEMATIC APPROACH

Although simple to grasp intellectually, strategic marketing planning is notoriously the most difficult of all marketing tasks. The reason why is that it involves bringing together into one coherent, realistic plan all the elements of marketing, and this 'coalescence' requires at least some degree of institutionalized procedures as well as inevitable compromise between conflicting objectives. For example, consider the four typical business objectives of: maximizing revenue; maximizing profits; maximizing return on investment; and minimizing costs. Each has its own special appeal to different managers within the organization, depending on their particular function. To achieve a kind of 'optimum compromise' demands accurate and collaborative understanding of how these variables interact, and steadfast rationality in decision-making.

Commercial success is, of course, influenced by many factors apart from just planning procedures. A myriad of contextual issues adds to the complexity of the marketing planning process. These include: company size; degree of internationalization; management style; degree of business environmental turbulence and competitive hostility; marketing growth rate; market share; technological developments; and so on. However, irrespective of the size or complexity of the organization, some kind of structured approach to situation analysis is necessary in order that meaningful and realistic marketing objectives can be set.

A frequent complaint is marketing's preoccupation with short-term thinking and an almost total lack of 'strategic thinking', or considering the longer-term implications of external and internal influences on the organization. Another complaint is that marketing plans consist largely of numbers, which bear little relationship to and offer little insight into current market position, key opportunities and threats, significant trends and issues, or indeed, how to meet sales targets. Financial objectives, while being essential measures of the desired performance of a company, are of scant practical help, since they say nothing about *how* the results are to be achieved. The same applies to sales forecasts and budgets, which are *not* marketing objectives and strategies. Basing company plans on a combination of forecasting and budgeting systems can only work if the future is going to be the same as the present or the past. As this is rarely the case, reliance on a forecasting and budgeting approach often leads to the following common problems:

- lost opportunities for profit;
- meaningless numbers in long-term plans;
- unrealistic objectives;
- lack of actionable market information;
- interfunctional strife;
- management frustration;
- proliferation of products and markets;
- wasted promotional expenditure;
- confusion over pricing;
- growing vulnerability to changes in the business environment;
- loss of control over the business.

These problems are symptomatic of a much deeper problem emanating from a lack of marketing planning. Marketing planning is about marketing objectives (*what* you want to achieve) and marketing strategies (*how* you plan to achieve your marketing objectives). There can be objectives and strategies at all levels in marketing. For example, there can be advertising objectives and strategies, and pricing objectives and strategies. However, it is important to remember that marketing objectives are confined to products and markets only. And they should be capable of measurement, otherwise they are not objectives. Measurement should be in terms of some or all of: sales volume, sales value, market share, profit, or percentage penetration of outlets.

Marketing objectives are confined to products and markets only

Marketing objectives are about one or more of the following:

- existing products in existing markets;
- new products for existing markets;
- existing products for new markets;
- new products for new markets.

Marketing strategies are the means by which marketing objectives will be achieved and are generally concerned with the four 'P's of the marketing mix: product, price, place and promotion.

Marketing strategies are the means by which marketing objectives will be achieved

Understanding the real meaning and significance of marketing objectives helps managers to know what information they need to enable them to think through the implications of choosing one or more positions in the market. However, finding the right words to describe the logic of marketing objectives and strategies is infinitely more difficult than writing down numbers on a piece of paper and leaving the strategies implicit. A numbers-orientated system will not encourage managers to think in a structured way about strategically relevant market segments, nor will it encourage the collection, analysis and synthesis of actionable market data. And in the absence of such activities within the organization, it is unlikely that the decision-makers will have much other than intuition and 'feel' to go on in determining how best to manage limited, valuable resources.

The challenge remains of how to get managers throughout an organization to think beyond the horizon of the current year's operations. Managers who are rewarded on the basis of current operational performance find it difficult to concern themselves about the corporate future. This is exacerbated by behavioural issues, in the sense that it is safer and more rewarding personally for managers to do what they know best, which, in most cases, is to manage their current range of products and customers in order to make the current year's budget.

Einstein wrote: 'The formulation of a problem is far more essential than its solution, which may be merely a matter of mathematical or experimental skill. To raise new questions, new possibilities, to regard old problems from a new perspective, requires creative imagination.' Unfortunately, in situations of problems old or new, such creativity is rare, especially when most managers are totally absorbed in managing today's business. Accordingly, they need some system that will help them think in a structured way about problem formulation, which in turn, can lead them to more effective problem resolution, and ideally to pre-empting and preventing problems in future.

The benefits of a marketing plan are that it:

- achieves better coordination of activities;
- identifies expected developments;

- increases organizational preparedness to change;
- minimizes non-rational responses to the unexpected;
- reduces conflicts about where the organization should be going;
- improves communications;
- forces management to think ahead systematically;
- enhances the matching of available resources to selected opportunities;
- provides a framework for the continuing review of operations;
- demands a systematic approach to strategy formulation, which leads to a higher return on investment.

There are four main stages in the marketing planning process: analysis, objectives, strategy, tactics. This process is formally expressed in two marketing plans, the strategic marketing plan and the tactical marketing plan.

Four main stages: analysis, objectives, strategy, tactics

THE DIFFERENCE BETWEEN STRATEGY AND TACTICS

The crux of marketing planning lies in knowing the difference between strategy and tactics. All organizations need to have a longer-term (strategic) marketing view as well as a short-term (tactical) marketing operation. Much of the confusion surrounding marketing planning derives predominantly from not understanding the real significance of a strategic marketing plan as opposed to a tactical, or operational marketing plan. A strategic marketing plan is for a period that extends beyond the next fiscal year, and usually covers three to five years. It is the backdrop against which operational decisions are taken, determining where the company is, where it wants to go and how it can get there. A tactical plan is for a shorter period, normally for one year or less. While similar in content, its level of detail is much greater as it contains the scheduling and costing of the specific actions necessary for the achievement of the first year of the strategic plan.

Tactical marketing plans should never be completed before strategic marketing plans

Tactical marketing plans should *never* be completed before strategic marketing plans. Most managers prefer selling the products they find easiest to sell to the customers that offer the least line of resistance. However, those who prepare tactical plans first and then extrapolate them merely succeed in extrapolating their own shortcomings. Such preoccupation with short-term plans is a typical mistake of companies that confuse sales forecasting and budgeting with strategic marketing planning.

The pragmatic, profit-related reasons for needing to develop a strategic marketing plan, and for doing so before deciding operational courses of action, are illustrated by the 'survival matrix' shown in Figure 1.1. The horizontal axis represents strategy as a continuum from ineffective to effective, while the vertical axis represents tactics on a continuum from inefficient to efficient. Those firms with an effective strategy and efficient tactics continue to thrive, while those with an effective strategy but inefficient tactics merely survive. Those firms to the left of the matrix are destined to die.

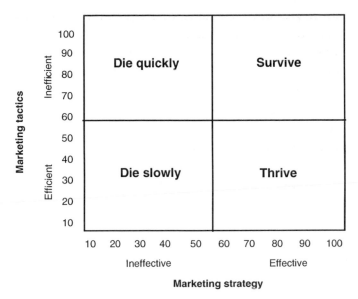

Figure 1.1   Survival matrix

To test your understanding of marketing planning, the business benefits it offers and the business realities it illuminates, complete Tests 1.1 and 1.2. (Test 1.2 utilizes Figure 1.2.)

Test 1.1: The benefits of marketing planning

Instructions
What follows is a list of the benefits of marketing planning. With your company in mind, score each benefit by means of the scale given below.

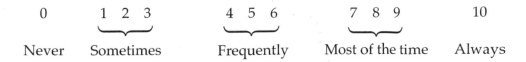

These tests are taken from *Marketing Plans: How to prepare them; how to use them,* Malcolm McDonald, Butterworth-Heinemann, Oxford, 6th edition, 2007

1. Our approach to marketing planning ensures that we get a high level of coordination of our various marketing activities. ( )
2. Our marketing planning process enables us to identify unexpected developments in advance. ( )
3. Because of the way we approach marketing planning, there is an increased readiness for the organization to change, in response to the issues 'flagged up'. ( )
4. When we are faced with the unexpected, our marketing planning process minimizes the risk of non-rational responses. ( )
5. Having a marketing plan reduces the conflicts between managers regarding 'where the company should be going'. ( )
6. Our marketing plan improves communications about market-related issues. ( )
7. Because of our marketing planning process, management is forced to think ahead systematically. ( )
8. Having a marketing plan enables us to match our resources to opportunities in an effective way. ( )
9. Our marketing plan provides us with a useful framework for a continuing review of progress. ( )
10. Our marketing planning has led us to develop more profitable marketing strategies. ( )

TOTAL _____

Scoring and interpretation for Test 1.1

The maximum score for the exercise is 100. If you scored:

81–100: Marketing planning is really paying off in your company.
61–80: You are not receiving the benefits you should be receiving.
41–60: You appear to be moving along the right lines, but there is still a long way to go.
0–40: Either your marketing planning process is inadequate, or your company is not really trying to make marketing planning work.

Test 1.2: The survival matrix

It is important to remember that profitability and high market growth are nearly always correlated. In other words, the higher the market growth, the higher the profitability.

This phenomenon can sometimes obscure the fact that a company that appears to be doing well can still be losing ground in comparison with its competitors. While apparently thriving, it is in fact dying slowly. The crunch comes when the erstwhile buoyant market growth slows down, and the other companies demonstrate quite clearly their superior performance.

Instructions

Before coming to the survival matrix, please respond to the following statements by scoring them as follows:

0	1 2 3	4 5 6	7 8 9	10
Never	Sometimes	Frequently	Most of the time	Always

1. We review our sales forecasts and budgets a minimum of once a month. (   )
2. The training we provide for salespeople is very good. (   )
3. Our salespeople consistently meet or exceed their sales targets. (   )
4. Any sales promotional campaigns we run are carefully monitored. (   )
5. We have a good relationship with our advertising agency. (   )
6. Our sales staff are clear about the role they are expected to play. (   )
7. Our sales managers are very good motivators. (   )
8. Most of the company knows who our best customers are. (   )
9. The sales force has a good conversion rate in terms of number of visits per order. (   )
10. Our marketing is reasonably stable, ie there is not a staff turnover problem. (   )

TOTAL _____

Scoring and interpretation for Test 1.2

Often the most potent short-term tactic is the use of the sales force. Following the example shown in Figure 1.2, enter the sales force effectiveness score on the vertical axis on the survival matrix (Figure 1.1) and then draw a horizontal dotted line across the matrix. Take the marketing benefits score from Test 1.1 and enter this on the horizontal axis of the matrix. Draw a vertical dotted line up from this point. Where the two dotted lines meet is where you position your company on the survival matrix.

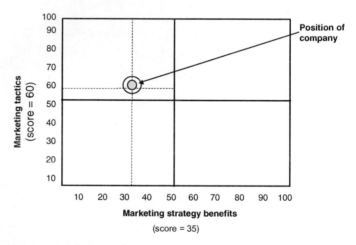

Figure 1.2 Positioning on the survival matrix

Questions

What are the implications for your company?
What actions might be required if improvements are needed?

QUESTIONS AND ANSWERS

Questions

1. In which century could it be said that the marketing concept was first advocated in a reasoned manner?
   a) 17th century
   b) 18th century
   c) 19th century
   d) 20th century

2. Marketing involves making both strategic and tactical decisions. Identify which are which by writing S (strategic) or T (tactical) in the brackets after the following.
   i) Decide to put emphasis on face-to-face selling. ( )
   ii) Set tougher sales targets. ( )
   iii) Run a sales promotion. ( )
   iv) Develop a new image for the company. ( )
   v) Reposition the product in the market. ( )
   vi) Change packaging colour. ( )

3. What does the marketing concept really mean?
   a) That the organization treats its customers in a friendly way.
   b) That the organization sets out to dominate a market.
   c) That the organization is driven by a desire to satisfy customer needs.
   d) That the organization sells its products more persuasively.

4. Which of the following is the most apt description of the marketing process?

a) A democratic process in which consumers have the right to select their preferred candidates (suppliers). They 'elect' them by casting their money votes to those who supply the goods or services that best satisfy their needs.

b) Deciding what the customer wants, arranging to make it, then distributing and selling it at a profit.

c) The planning and execution of all business activities so that the optimum influence is exerted on the customer, resulting in an optimization of prices and greater long-term profits.

d) The organization and performance of those business activities which facilitate the exchange of goods and services between the maker and the user.

5. Two competing banks in the same town offer much the same range of financial products. Research has revealed that 80 per cent of bank customers in the town have a preference for telephone or online banking. Even so, Bank A decides to extend its opening hours.

How should Bank B respond? Should it:

a) Do nothing different?
b) Copy Bank A's opening hours?
c) Open for even longer than Bank A?
d) Do market research on the effectiveness of its current opening hours?

6. Which of the following is NOT part of the marketing mix?
    a) customer service   d) price
    b) research and development   e) distribution
    c) advertising

7. Which of the following is NOT an organizational capability?
    a) creativity   d) environmental concern
    b) technology   e) compliance with ISO 9000
    c) skilled labour   (International Quality
                            Standard)
                        f) research and development

8. Which of the following is NOT part of the business environment?
    a) legislation   f) technological
    b) trading standards   developments
    c) market trends   g) competition
    d) market share   h) fashion
    e) economic trends

9. Marketing literature is liberally sprinkled with the words 'customers' and 'markets'. Which of the following statements do you believe is most accurate?
    a) 'Customers' and 'markets' mean the same thing.
    b) 'Customers' are real, 'markets' are what we define them to be.
    c) 'Customers' come and go, but 'markets' remain.
    d) Look after 'customers' and 'markets' will look after themselves.

10. It is said that the marketing planning process has to be appropriate for the organization. Which of the following appears to be the best fit?
    a) Small company with a limited range uses a highly formal process.
    b) Large company with several operating units uses a highly centralized planning process.
    c) Large company with complex range of products uses a semi-formal process.
    d) Small company with wide-range in a single market uses a very informal planning process.

Answers

Question 1 Adam Smith, *The Wealth of Nations*, 1776.
Answer = b).

Question 2 Remember a strategic decision needs time to bear fruit, a tactical decision can make immediate impact.
Answer: i) = S, ii) = T, iii) = T, iv) = S, v) = S, vi) = T.

Question 3 While a), b) and d) might sound reasonable, c) is the true answer.
Answer = c).

Question 4 It is the only definition that reflects the 'matching' of supplier's capabilities with the satisfaction of the buyer's needs.
Answer = a).

Question 5   To copy what competitors do, without having good reason, is to invite costs to escalate and get nothing back in return.
Answer = d).

Question 6   Although research and development may contribute to new product development eventually, it does not constitute being part of the marketing mix.
Answer = b).

Question 7   Having a concern for something (conceptual) is not the same as being good at something (actual).
Answer = d).

Question 8   Market share is a measure of how well the company is meeting the needs of a specific market segment. It is not an environmental factor.
Answer = d).

Question 9   Customers are certainly real but we can define our markets by industry, geography, customer types, etc. Markets are not static and not all customers will fall into the same segments.
Answer = b).

Question 10   a) = overkill, b) = too controlled, c) = too informal.
Answer = d).

2

How marketing planning fits with corporate planning

Marketing planning is the means by which an organization monitors and controls the many internal and external influences on its ability to achieve profitable sales, and communicates throughout its ranks the competitive stance it has chosen to achieve its objectives. It is therefore not possible to plan an organization's marketing activities in isolation from other business functions. Consequently, the marketing planning process should be firmly based on a corporate planning system.

A business starts at some time with resources and wants to use those resources to achieve something. This desired destination, or result, is a corporate objective. Most often corporate objectives are expressed in terms of profit, since profit is the means of satisfying shareholders or owners, and because it is one universally accepted criterion by

It is not possible to plan marketing activities in isolation from other business functions which efficiency can be evaluated, which will in turn lead to efficient resource allocation, economic and technical progressiveness and stability. The policies an organization adopts to pursue its profit objectives, such as to compete in a market, to manufacture itself but to outsource distribution, to manage within cash flow and so on, are corporate strategies.

In practice, companies tend to operate by way of functional divisions, each with a separate identity, so that what is a strategy in the corporate plan becomes an objective within each department. For example, marketing strategies within the corporate plan become operating objectives within the marketing department, and strategies at the general level within the marketing department become operating objectives at the next level down (eg, advertising, sales promotion, personal selling). At the further level down, there would be, say, advertising objectives and advertising strategies, with the subsequent programmes and budgets for achieving the objectives. In this way, a hierarchy of objectives and strategies is formed, which can be traced back to the initial corporate objective.

A hierarchy of objectives and strategies

The really important point, apart from clarifying the difference between objectives and strategies, is that the further down the hierarchical chain one goes, the less likely it is that a stated objective will make a cost-effective contribution to company profits, unless it derives logically and directly from an objective at a higher level. Thus meaningful marketing objectives, concerning what is sold (products/services) and to whom it is sold (its markets), will relate directly to corporate objectives, or the desired level of profit the organization seeks to achieve.

While marketing planning is based on markets, customers and products/services, business planning involves other corporate resources, which will have a bearing on the identified markets. It is therefore useful to understand how marketing planning relates to the corporate planning process. There are five steps in the corporate planning process, as outlined in Figure 2.1.

Step 1 amounts to a statement of corporate financial objectives for the long-range planning period of the organization. These objectives are often expressed in terms of turnover, profit before tax, and return on investment. Usually this planning horizon is five years, but the precise period should be determined by the nature of the markets in which the organization operates. A useful guideline is that there should be a market for the organization's products for long enough at least to amortize any capital investment associated with those products. It is advisable to keep the period down to three years, since beyond this period any detail in the strategic plan is likely to become pointless.

Corporate planning: step 1 – corporate financial objectives

Step 2 is an audit, or systematic, critical and unbiased review and appraisal of the environment and the company's operations. In practice, the best way to carry out a management audit is to conduct a separate audit of each major management function. Thus the marketing audit (concerned with the marketing environment and marketing operations) is part of the larger management audit, in the same way that the operations audit is.

Corporate planning: step 2 – management audit

Step 3, objective and strategy setting, is undoubtedly the most important and difficult of the corporate planning stages, since if this is not done properly everything that follows is of little value.

Corporate planning: step 3 – objective and strategy setting

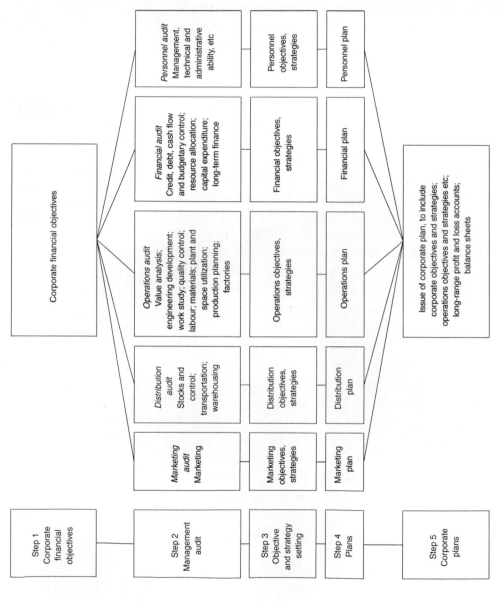

Figure 2.1 Marketing planning within the corporate planning process

This is the stage in the planning cycle when a compromise had to be reached between what is wanted by the several functional departments and what is practicable given the constraints within which any organization operates.

Step 4 involves producing detailed plans for one year, containing the responsibilities, timing and costs of carrying out the first year's objectives, and broad plans for the following years.

Corporate planning: step 4 – step plans

Step 5 is an incorporation of these detailed plans into a corporate plan, which will contain long-range corporate objectives, strategies, plans, profit and loss accounts, and balance sheets. A main purpose of the corporate plan is to provide a long-term vision of what the company is or is striving to become, taking account of shareholder expectations, both resource and consumption market trends, and the distinctive competence of the organization as revealed by the management audit.

Corporate planning: step 5 – corporate plans

What this means in practice is that the corporate plan will contain at least the following elements:

- Corporate objective, or the desired level of profitability.
- Corporate strategies, which denote business boundaries
  - what kinds of products will be sold to what kinds of markets (marketing)
  - what kinds of facilities will be developed (operations and distribution)
  - the size and character of the labour force (personnel)
  - funding (finance).

- Other corporate objectives, such as social responsibility, corporate/stock market/employer image, etc.

Linking the corporate plan to the marketing plan

The relevance of the corporate plan to the marketing plan is immediately visible in that the first item to appear in the marketing plan is often a page outlining the corporate mission and objectives. It should consist of brief statements about the organization's role or contribution, business definition, distinctive competences, and indications for the future (ie, what the firm will do, might do, will never do). The mission statement should be followed with a section summarizing the organization's financial performance, and its financial projections for the three-year planning period. This will provide the person reading the marketing plan with an overview of the financial implications of the plan, including the organization's financial goals (revenue and profit targets) and how these will be achieved. The mission statement and financial summary represent the goal-setting phase of the marketing planning process, ensuring that the marketing plan is launched on a firm and realistic corporate footing.

QUESTIONS AND ANSWERS

Questions

1. Which of the following is NOT a corporate objective?
   a) To make 15 per cent return on capital employed.
   b) To be the most profitable company in our

market sector as measured by return on net assets.
c) To increase earnings per share by x per cent per annum.
d) To improve customer service levels by x per cent per annum.

2. Which of the following is NOT a marketing objective?
   a) To sell N products to segment A.
   b) To generate £Y from segment B.
   c) To increase market share of product X in segment C.
   d) To increase prices by 10 per cent.

3. The objective-setting process of a company ought to be primarily based on:
   a) Previous sales records.
   b) Its markets.
   c) Maximizing profits.
   d) Its productive resources.

4. A mission statement is intended to:
   a) Make all employees feel good about the business.
   b) Describe in detail the core strengths of the company.
   c) Highlight the role of the business, its distinctive competence, future direction and motivate the employees.
   d) Be a 'call to arms', eg 'we are going to wipe out our competitors'.

5. Here are two sets of 'snapshots' taken of four companies over a three-year period. Which one looks to have the most successful future?

	A	B	C	D
3 years ago				
Sales revenue (£m)	250	150	200	180
Net profit (£m)	16	17	10	15
Return on assets %	12	18	8	12
Market growth %	18	22	12	15
Market share %	20	15	18	15
Today				
Sales revenue (£M)	450	140	220	300
Net profit (£M)	55	15	12	25
Return on assets %	26	20	14	18
Market growth %	17.5	15	19	18
Market share %	9	14	19	20

6. In identifying what makes a key account customer should you consider:
   a) The people at each customer account and their relationship with you.
   b) A range of factors which would make a customer attractive to your company.
   c) The price you can get for your products.
   d) The volume of sales you have with a customer.

7. Several factors inhibit the marketing planning process. Which of the following is not such a factor?
   a) An over-reliance on numbers and detail.
   b) Confusion over marketing planning terms.
   c) The separation of strategic and tactical plans.
   d) The involvement of non-marketing managers.

8. Creativity is said to be a vital component of marketing. In which type of organizational setting is it most likely to flourish productively?
   a) An organization which plans ahead realistically and sets very challenging targets.
   b) An organization with a highly autocratic CEO.
   c) A bureaucratic organization.
   d) A 'laissez-faire' organization where staff have considerable freedom to act.

9. Market research should be used to:
   a) Confirm the action you have taken (eg build new plant, investment, etc).
   b) Enable critical business decisions to be made with confidence.
   c) Demonstrate to customers that you care about their reaction to new products and services offered by your company.
   d) Examine market possibilities to identify trends and market opportunities for your business.

10. Which of the following is more likely to result in long-term success?
    a) Making customers aware of your products and their benefits.
    b) Paying high salaries to product managers.

    c) Developing first-class products (which will sell themselves).

    d) Setting a high price (to maximize profits).

Answers

Question 1   Answer = d). This is a customer service objective.

Question 2   Answer = d). This is a pricing objective.

Question 3   It is only by understanding its markets that a company can be successful. Answer = b).

Question 4   While there is some merit in answers a), b) and d) – although with d) there may be some question marks – c) is the main reason to have a mission statement. Answer = c).

Question 5   Company A has increased revenue and profits but market is not growing and share is declining rapidly. B and C have not changed significantly. C is doing slightly better. D has increased revenue and profits and market growth and market share are up. Answer = d).

Question 6   Not only is this true for now, but it must also be true (ie attractive) in the future. Answer = b).

Question 7   Answer = d). It is often helpful if colleagues get involved.

Question 8   To some d) may look to be an attractive answer, but constructive creativity comes from the organizational brain-power being focused on real issues, not from everybody doing 'their own thing'. b) is dismissed because auto-cratic CEOs rarely welcome the ideas of others. In bureaucratic organizations (c), the operational procedures (red tape) tend to discourage any lateral thinking.
Answer = a).

Question 9   Answer = d).

Question 10 Answer = a).

3

The strategic marketing planning process and the marketing plan

As mentioned earlier, the strategic marketing planning process is a series of logical steps that have to be worked through in order to arrive at a marketing plan. Strategic marketing planning by means of a planning system is, *per se*, little more than a structured way of identifying a range of options for the company, of making them explicit in writing, of formulating marketing objectives which are consistent with the company's overall objectives and of scheduling and costing out the specific activities most likely to bring about the achievement of the objectives. It is the systemization of this process which is distinctive and which lies at the heart of the theory of strategic marketing planning.

Figure 3.1 outlines the constituent 10 steps, highlighting the difference between the *process* of marketing planning and its output, the actual

Logical steps to marketing planning

written marketing *plan*. A more comprehensive description of the 'ingredients' and 'recipe' for producing a strategic marketing plan is provided at the end of this chapter.

Experience has shown that a strategic marketing plan should contain: a mission statement; financial summary; market overview; SWOT analyses; assumptions; marketing objectives and strategies appropriately prioritized; and resource allocations containing details of timings, responsibilities and costs, with forecasts and budgets. To ensure that these elements appear in the marketing plan, it is necessary to complete each of the first nine planning steps in succession before producing the detailed one-year plan. However, the dotted lines in Figure 3.1 indicate the reality of the marketing planning process, that is to say, it is likely that each of these steps will have to be gone through more than once before final marketing programmes can be written.

An iterative process

The initial, goal-setting phase of the marketing planning process was considered in Chapter 2, where it was emphasized that the clear definition of agreed corporate objectives and organizational mission is fundamental to the success of marketing planning, and consequently, to the success of the marketing plan. This chapter proceeds to describe the importance and activity of the second phase, the situation review.

MARKETING AUDIT

Clearly, any marketing plan will only be as good as the information on which it is based, and the marketing audit is the means by which information

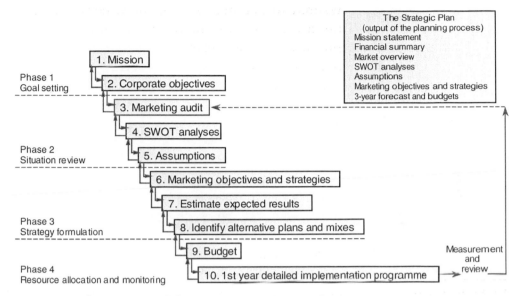

Figure 3.1 The 10 steps of the strategic marketing planning process

for planning is organized. A marketing audit is a systematic, critical and unbiased review and appraisal of all the external and internal factors that have affected an organization's commercial performance over a defined period. It answers the question: 'Where is the organization now?' The marketing audit is essentially a database of all market-related issues for the company, which forms part of the company-wide management audit. By providing an understanding of how the organization relates to the environment in which it operates, the marketing audit enables management to select a position within that environment based on known factors.

Often the need for a marketing audit does not manifest itself until things start to go wrong for the organization, such as declining sales, falling margins, lost market share, under-utilized production capacity, and so on. However, without knowing the cause of these danger signs, management can easily treat the wrong symptoms and fail to address the root problems. For example, the introduction of new products, restructuring of the sales force, reduction of prices or cutting of costs are unlikely to be effective measures if more fundamental problems have not been identified. Of course, if the organization survived for long enough, it might eventually solve its problems though a process of elimination. Either way, the problems have first to be properly defined, and the marketing audit helps to define them by providing a structured approach to the collection and analysis of data and information on the complex business environment.

Any organization carrying out an audit will be faced with two kinds of variable: those over which it has no direct control and those over which it has complete control. The former include economic and market factors, while the latter usually concern the organization's resources, or operational variables.

Marketing audit: external audit and internal audit

This division suggests that the marketing audit should be structured in two parts:

- External audit – the uncontrollable variables (business and economic environment, the market, the competition).
- Internal audit – the controllable variables (organization's strengths and weaknesses, operations and resources vis-à-vis the environment and competitors).

The key areas that should be investigated under these two headings are outlined in Table 3.1.

As well as considering *what* the marketing audit should cover, *when* the audit should be undertaken

Table 3.1 The marketing audit checklist

External audit
Business and economic environment
  – political / fiscal / legal
  – economic
  – social / cultural
  – technological
  – intra-company

The market
Total market, size, growth and trends (value / volume)
Market characteristics, developments and trends
  – products
  – prices
  – physical distribution
  – channels
  – customers / consumers
  – communication
  – industry practices

Competition
Major competitors
Size
Market share / coverage
Market standing / reputation
Production capabilities
Distribution policies
Marketing methods
Extent of diversification
Personal issues
International links
Profitability
Key strengths and weaknesses

Internal audit
marketing operational variables

Own company
Sales (total, by geographical location, industrial
Type, customer, by product)
Market shares
Profit margins / costs
Marketing mix variables as follows:
  – product management
  – price
  – distribution
  – promotion
  – operations and resources

and *who* should undertake it are also crucial to the effectiveness of the resulting marketing plan. Many people hold the mistaken belief that the marketing audit should be a last-ditch attempt to define an organization's marketing problems, or at best something done by an independent body from time to time to ensure that an organization is on the right track. However, since marketing is such a complex function, it seems illogical not to carry out a pretty thorough situation analysis at least once a year at the beginning of the planning cycle (described in Chapter 12). Many highly successful companies, in addition to using normal information and control procedures and marketing research throughout the year, also undertake an annual self-audit of everything that has had an important influence on marketing activities as a discipline integrated into the management process.

Successful companies undertake annual self-audit

This can be achieved, firstly, by institutionalizing procedures in as much detail as possible so that all managers involved in the audit, from the highest to the lowest levels, conform to a disciplined approach; and secondly, by providing thorough training in the use of the procedures themselves.

SWOT ANALYSES

The next task is to turn the results of the marketing audit into actionable intelligence. It is essential at this stage to concentrate on analysis that determines which trends and developments will actually affect the organization, and to omit all the information that is not central to the organization's marketing problems. Inclusion of over-detailed sales performance histories by product, for instance, which lead to no logical actions whatever, only serve to rob the audit of focus and reduce its relevance.

Since the purpose of the marketing audit is to indicate what the organization's marketing objectives and strategies should be, it is helpful to adopt a format for organizing the audit's major findings. A useful way of doing this is to complete a SWOT (strengths, weaknesses, opportunities, threats) analysis for each major product or market segment. A SWOT is a summary listing of internal *differential* strengths and weaknesses vis-à-vis competitors and *key* external opportunities and threats. It should include reasons for good or poor performance. By identifying the critical success factors (CSFs) for the organization, and important outside influences and their implications, the key issues to be addressed will emerge.

A SWOT is a summary of internal differential strengths and weaknesses vis-à-vis competitors and key external opportunities and threats

A SWOT should answer such questions as:

- What do customers need?
- How do they buy?
- What are our competitors doing?
- How well are we performing against customer needs?
- What are the key opportunities and threats?

A SWOT should be brief, interesting and concise, if possible, running to no more than two pages. It is generated from internal debate and is not just one person's opinion. The SWOTs should enable the reader, whether or not he or she was involved in their preparation, to grasp instantly the main thrust of the business, even to the point of being able to write marketing objectives. It is important to remember that only the SWOT analyses, *not* the audit, will actually appear in the marketing plan.

A sample form for SWOT analysis, leading to strategy formulation, is given in Figure 3.2. This form should be completed for each of the organization's market segments.

ASSUMPTIONS

Having completed the marketing audit and SWOT analyses, fundamental assumptions on future conditions can be made relating to each product/market segment under consideration. These assumptions will also appear in the marketing plan. An example of a written assumption might be: 'With respect to the company's industrial climate, it is assumed that industrial overcapacity will increase from 105 per cent to 115 per cent as new industrial plants come into operation, price competition will force price levels down by 10 per cent across the board; a new product will be introduced by our major competitor before the end of the second quarter'.

Assumptions: external factors beyond your control

Assumptions should be key and few in number. If the plan can be implemented irrespective of the assumption, then the assumption is unnecessary. As a measure of their importance, these assumptions will be used to guide the setting of marketing objectives and strategies.

STRATEGY FORMULATION

Strategy formulation will involve estimating expected results, and considering alternative ways forward and marketing mixes. When the strategies

1. SEGMENT DESCRIPTION
It should be a specific part of the business and should be very important to the organization

2. CRITICAL SUCCESS FACTORS (CSFs)
What are the few key things from the customers' point of view that any competitor has to do right to succeed

1
2
3
4
5

3. WEIGHTING
How important is each of these CSFs? Score out of 100

Total 100

4. STRENGTHS/WEAKNESSES ANALYSIS
Score yourself and each of your main competitors out of 10 on each of the CSFs. Then multiply the score by the weight.

	You	Comp A	Comp B	Comp C	Comp D
1					
2					
3					
4					
5					
Total					

5. OPPORTUNITIES / THREATS
What are the few things outside your direct control that have had, and will have, an impact on this part of your business?

OPPORTUNITIES

1
2
3
4
5

THREATS

1
2
3
4
5

6. KEY ISSUES THAT NEED TO BE ADDRESSED
What are the really key issues from the SWOT that need to be addressed?

1
2
3
4
5

Figure 3.2 Sample form for SWOT analysis

have been agreed, the resources and activities required to deliver the strategies need to be costed out, resulting in the budget. Finally, a one-year tactical plan (first year detailed implementation programme) must be developed, turning the general marketing strategies into specific sub-objectives, each supported by more detailed strategy and action statements. Depending on the circumstances, this might comprise an advertising plan, a sales promotion plan, a pricing plan, a product plan, and so on, or any combination thereof.

STRATEGIC MARKETING PLAN 'INGREDIENTS' AND 'RECIPE'

Figure 3.3 is a summary of what appears in a strategic marketing plan ('ingredients'), together with a list of the principal marketing tools/techniques/structures/frameworks that apply to each step in the marketing planning process. Table 3.2 outlines the successive actions ('recipe') required to produce a strategic marketing plan. These should be borne in mind throughout the remainder of the book, and may be usefully revisited for clarification and instruction.

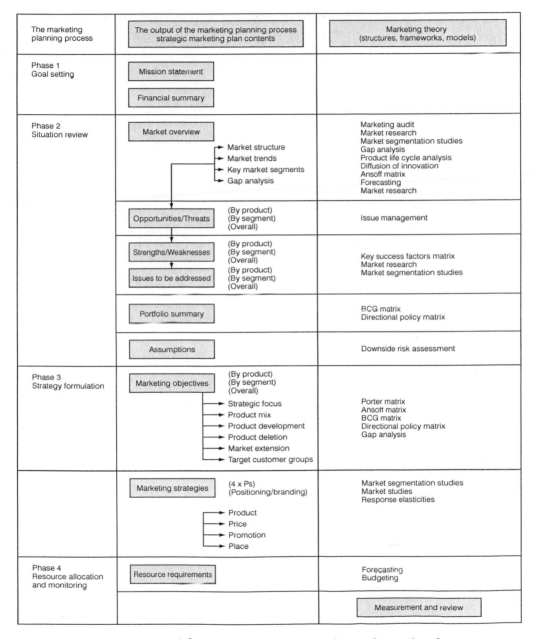

The marketing planning process	The output of the marketing planning process strategic marketing plan contents		Marketing theory (structures, frameworks, models)
Phase 1 Goal setting	Mission statement		
	Financial summary		
Phase 2 Situation review	Market overview		Marketing audit Market research Market segmentation studies Gap analysis Product life cycle analysis Diffusion of innovation Ansoff matrix Forecasting Market research
		→ Market structure → Market trends → Key market segments ↳ Gap analysis	
	Opportunities/Threats	(By product) (By segment) (Overall)	Issue management
	Strengths/Weaknesses	(By product) (By segment) (Overall)	Key success factors matrix Market research Market segmentation studies
	Issues to be addressed	(By product) (By segment) (Overall)	
	Portfolio summary		BCG matrix Directional policy matrix
	Assumptions		Downside risk assessment
Phase 3 Strategy formulation	Marketing objectives	(By product) (By segment) (Overall)	
		→ Strategic focus → Product mix → Product development → Product deletion → Market extension ↳ Target customer groups	Porter matrix Ansoff matrix BCG matrix Directional policy matrix Gap analysis
	Marketing strategies	(4 x Ps) (Positioning/branding)	Market segmentation studies Market studies Response elasticities
		→ Product → Price → Promotion ↳ Place	
Phase 4 Resource allocation and monitoring	Resource requirements		Forecasting Budgeting
			Measurement and review

Figure 3.3 'Ingredients' of the strategic marketing plan and associated tools/techniques

Table 3.2 'Recipe' for producing a strategic marketing plan

1. Start with a mission or purpose statement.
2. Include a financial summary that illustrates graphically revenue and profit for the full planning period.
3. Carry out a market overview:
   - What *is* the market?
   - Has the market declined or grown?
   - How does it break down into segments?
   - What are the trends in each?
4. Identify the key segments and do a SWOT analysis for each one:
   - Outline the major external influences and their impact on each segment.
   - List the key factors for success. There should be less than five or six.
   - Give an assessment of the company's differential strengths and weaknesses compared with those of its competitors'. (Score yourself and your competitors out of 10 and then multiply each score by a weighting factor for each critical success factor, eg, CSF1 = 60, CSF2 = 25, CSF3 = 10, CSF4 = 5.)
5. Make a brief statement about the key issues that have to be addressed in the planning period.
6. Summarize the SWOTs using a portfolio matrix in order to illustrate the important relationships between the key points of your business.
7. List your assumptions.
8. Set objectives and strategies.
9. Summarize your resource requirements for the planning period in the form of a budget.

QUESTIONS AND ANSWERS

Questions

1. The process of strategic marketing planning is concerned with:
   a) Identifying which customers get which products in the long term.
   b) Selling what the company can produce most economically.
   c) Forecasting future sales and budgeting to meet them.
   d) Identifying to whom sales will be made in the short term.

2. In carrying out a SWOT analysis you should:
   a) First examine your weaknesses.
   b) First examine your external environment to identify your strengths.
   c) First examine the external environment to see what opportunities and threats exist.
   d) Carry out a situation review to identify by segment, relative strengths, weaknesses, opportunities and threats.

3. A consultant identifies a lack of marketing planning in a client company. What would be his or her best strategy to move things forward?
   a) Write the first marketing plan himself or herself, as a model to be followed.
   b) Enthuse the CEO about marketing planning.
   c) Run training sessions for managers about marketing planning.
   d) Set up a marketing information system.

4. In what context should markets/customers and products/services be used?
   a) To establish the company's competitive position.
   b) To aid forecasting.
   c) To set marketing objectives and strategies.
   d) To select the best marketing option.

5. How important are assumptions in the planning process? Which of the following is most accurate?
   a) Having assumptions is a lazy way of avoiding finding out the facts. They weaken the process.
   b) It is OK to have assumptions, as long as they are realistic and few in number.
   c) Every assumption you make ought to be noted so that you cannot be blamed if things go wrong.
   d) It is not necessary to note assumptions in the plan because it will be obvious where they have been made.

6. Here are four rationales for planning. Which is most consistent with strategic marketing?
   a) Plan to survive first, then take it from there.
   b) Plan to be thriving in three years' time.
   c) Plan to meet the annual sales forecast.
   d) Plan to respond quickly to sudden opportunities.

7. Which of these outcomes is most likely in the short term when a company introduces marketing planning?
   a) It will immediately become successful.
   b) The corporate culture will change.

  c) It will create a competitive advantage.
  d) It will cause the business to reappraise its
     priorities.

8. The basic marketing planning process is drawn
   below, but some of the steps are missing. Your
   task is to fill in the blanks.

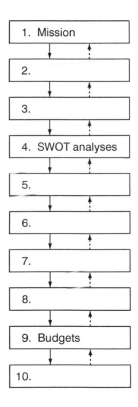

9. A marketing audit is:
   a) A comprehensive description of the market-place.
   b) A detailed analysis of the customer database.
   c) An analysis of the company's marketing performance in the context of industrial trends and changes in the marketing environment.
   d) An analysis of company's strengths and weaknesses against the competition.

10. The SWOT analysis is intended to capture the key issues from the marketing audit. Here are some factors that might appear in such an audit. Mark in the brackets whether you think they are S (strength), W (weakness), O (opportunity), T (threat) or NS (not significant enough to be included in the SWOT). There are two factors for each category.
   i) Two key account managers are not well trained ( )
   ii) Our main competitor is extending its product range. ( )
   iii) We have a patent on the product finishing process. ( )
   iv) Our level of customer service is about average for this industry. ( )
   v) Our customer retention ratio is rising. ( )
   vi) Our main competitor has had major problems with suppliers and fallen down on deliveries to customers. ( )
   vii) Interest rates are likely to remain stable. ( )
   viii) Tariff barriers are to be reduced in target export market. ( )

ix) Our product range is ageing.   (   )
x) Imported goods make an ever-
    increasing proportion of total sales in
    our market.   (   )

Answers

Question 1   This is most likely to ensure the organi-
             zation's long-term health.
             Answer = a).

Question 2   SWOTs are most useful when done by
             segment.
             Answer = d).

Question 3   Without the enthusiastic support of the
             CEO marketing planning is doomed to
             failure.
             Answer = b).

Question 4   Marketing objectives are about what is
             sold and to whom.
             Answer = c).

Question 5   When we are trying to look into the
             future we can only do so by making
             some assumptions. However, they
             ought to be significant and few in
             number, otherwise the plan is being
             built on quicksand.
             Answer = b).

Question 6   Strategic planning looks at a longer
             time scale.
             Answer = b).

Question 7 The introduction of marketing planning invariably confronts managers with new data and hence new choices. What seemed good business yesterday does not necessarily stay that way in the light of a thorough marketing audit.
Answer = d).

Question 8 Answer: 2 = Corporate objectives, 3 = Marketing audit, 5 = Assumptions, 6 = Marketing objectives and strategies, 7 = Estimate expected results, 8 = Alternative plans and mixes, 10 = Detailed first year plan.

Question 9 a), b) and d) might figure as a part of the marketing audit but are not by themselves a market audit.
Answer = c).

Question 10 Answer: i) = W, ii) = T, iii) = S, iv) = NS, v) = S, vi) = O, vii) = NS, viii) = O, ix) = W, x) = T.

Before turning to the subject of strategy formulation, it is worth taking a closer look at the main components of the marketing audit, namely the customer and market audit and the product audit, which we do in Chapters 4 and 5.

4

Defining markets and segments prior to planning

One of the key aspects of marketing planning is choosing the right customers to focus on. Few companies can successfully be 'all things to all people', and it is therefore necessary to define in precise and actionable terms just who are the organization's customers, both now and in the future. Knowing where sales and profits are coming from is key to understanding current market positions and assessing potential market directions.

Choosing the right customers

Most companies experience a phenomenon called the Pareto effect, or the 80/20 rule, whereby some 20 per cent of customers account for 80 per cent of business. However, this does not mean that the best potential customers reside in the top fifth of the market, and care must be taken to identify and address each market segment appropriately in the context of the market as a whole.

Market segmentation enables a firm to target its limited resources on the most promising opportunities by sorting customers into economically manageable and 'prioritizable' groups. Segmentation can be based on a myriad of criteria regarding customer characteristics and buying behaviour, thus covering the critical issues of 'who buys', 'what they buy' and 'why they buy'. The bases for market segmentation are summarized as follows:

What is bought	Price categories, outlets used, physical characteristics of different products. Analysis of product and purchase characteristics clarifies market structure and market mechanics.
Who buys	Demographic/socio-economic/geographic/cultural factors. Analysis of customer attributes aids communication programme design.
Why	Benefits, attitudes/beliefs, personality/lifestyle. Analysis of customer behaviour underpins marketing strategy.

A market segment is a group of customers with similar requirements which can be satisfied by a distinct marketing mix

A market segment should be a group of customers with the same or similar requirements, which can be satisfied by a distinct marketing mix. The universally accepted criteria concerning what constitutes a viable market segment are:

- segments should be of an adequate size to provide the organization with the desired return for its effort;

- members of each segment should have a high degree of similarity in their requirements, yet be distinct from the rest of the market.

- criteria for describing segments must be relevant to the purchase situation;
- segments must be reachable.

A useful way of tackling the complex issue of market segmentation is to start by drawing a 'market map' as a precursor to a more detailed examination of who buys what. A market map defines the distribution and value chain between the supplier and the end user, or consumer, taking into account the various buying mechanisms found in a market, including the part played by 'influencers', or third parties that advise on or otherwise sway the outcome of the purchasing decision. Influencers should appear on the market map, as shown in Figure 4.1, just as if they were a transaction stage. By tracing the 'routes' of transactions in your market, it is possible to identify the most important routes, as well as the key junctions where decisions are made and segmentation could occur.

A 'market map' defines the distribution and value chain between the supplier and the end user

Key junctions where decisions are made is where segmentation should be considered

Clearly, the typology of the customer or the segment should be related to the firm's distinctive competence and that of its competitors – as identified in the marketing audit and SWOT analyses – if differential advantage is to be created. Remember, the purpose of segmentation is to find the best ways to

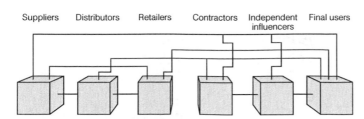

Suppliers Distributors Retailers Contractors Independent Final users
influencers

Figure 4.1 Market map with influencers

match the organization's capabilities with groups of customers who share similar needs, and thereby achieve some commercial gain. Marketers must also be aware that customers (people who buy from you) and consumers (users of your products or services) may not always be one and the same. For instance, a husband (customer/purchaser) buys perfume for his wife (consumer). To be an attractive proposition, the 'package' of benefits offered by the product/service will need to reflect the characteristics of both customer and consumer.

Customers and consumers

Customers buy products and services because they seek the benefits derived from them, not their inherent features. In this sense, products and services are problem solvers. For example, customers buy aspirin to solve the problem of headaches, and they buy drills because they need holes. Not every product or service benefit will have equal appeal to all customers, or groups of customers. However, through customer dialogue or market research it is possible to establish which benefits customers perceive as important.

To be useful for segmentation, a benefit has to appeal to a significant number of customers. Benefit analysis, or the listing of features of major products together with what they mean to the customer, is a way of identifying which are the most important benefits to which customers. To get from a feature to an advantage, and then to a benefit, the phrases 'which means that?' and 'so what?' can be helpful. For example, 'Our products are handmade by experts (feature), which means that they are better quality than machine-made ones' (advantage) – so what? – 'which means that they last longer' (the real benefit).

Feature – advantage – benefit

Obviously, the better your products/services provide benefits to customers which match their needs, the more competitive your products/services are going to be in the marketplace. Also, the more accurately you can define your market segments, the more accurately you can measure your market share. Correct market definition is crucial for:

- share measurement;
- growth measurement;
- the specification of target customers;
- the recognition of relevant competitors;
- the formulation of marketing objectives and strategies.

Market share is the proportion of *actual* sales (either volume or value) within a defined market, and is thus a measure of satisfying customers. A frequent mistake that is made by people who do not understand what market share really means is to assume that their company has only a small share of some market, whereas, if the company is commercially successful, it probably has a much larger share of a smaller market.

Considering the direct relationship between market share and profitability, it is important to arrive at a meaningful balance between a broad market definition and a manageable market definition. Too narrow a definition could restrict the range of new opportunities afforded through segmentation; too broad a definition could make marketing planning meaningless. A market is essentially the aggregation of all the alternative goods or services that customers regard as being capable of satisfying the same customer need. The following definitions can be useful in calculating market share:

A market is the aggregation of all the alternative goods or services capable of satisfying the same customer need

- product class, eg, cigarettes, computers, fertilizers, carpets;

- product sub-class, eg, filter, personal computers, nitrogen, carpet tiles;
- product brand, eg, Silk Cut, Dell, Nitram, Heuga.

The organization's ability to satisfy customers, especially major customers of strategic importance, or key accounts, on a consistent and continual basis is crucial to both customer acquisition and customer retention. Within any given market segment there are critical success factors (CSFs) for winning the business, such as breadth of offering, speed of service, low prices, reliable delivery, and so on. The secret of marketing success is, of course, to change the offer in accordance with changing needs, and not to offer exactly the same product or service to everyone. It is therefore essential for an organization to establish what these CSFs are *and* how well the organization compares with its closest competitors, when measured against these factors. Without such insight, the road to achieving sustainable competitive advantage will be unnecessarily difficult.

QUESTIONS AND ANSWERS

Questions

1. Below are a number of words. Your task is to fit them into the correct places in the table below. There are four sets of items to consider.

    Hoover, beer, lipstick, Subaru, upright vacuum cleaners, bitter, cosmetics, cars, Bass, vacuum cleaners, 4-wheel-drive, Revlon.

Product class				
Product sub-class				
Product brand				

2. Which of the below ought not to figure in the criteria for selecting a market segment? Segment is:
    a) Based on company product range.
    b) Sufficiently large to generate required revenue.
    c) Distinctly different.
    d) Reachable for communications.

3. Below is a blank marketing map. Using the following information, fill in the blank boxes, show quantities when you can, and put arrows showing direction.

    A farmer grows strawberries. About 10 per cent of his crop is sold to 'pick your own' enthusiasts and a similar quantity is sold in the farm shop. About 20 per cent of the crop is sold to a jam factory and the remainder goes to a wholesaler who distributes to shops, bakers and restaurants.

4. Here are some occupations. Write next to each

one if it falls into the socio-demographic class of A, B, C1, C2, D or E.

i) packer in factory	( )	vi)	office supervisor	( )
ii) partner in law firm	( )	vii)	wood carver	( )
iii) sales manager	( )	viii)	junior school teacher	( )
iv) snow clearer	( )	ix)	dentist	( )
v) plumber	( )	x)	Army general (retired)	( )

5. A differential benefit is:
   a) Different from other benefits you offer.
   b) Different from what you used to offer.
   c) Different from what competitors offer.
   d) Different from what the market expects.

6. A newly appointed marketing manager set out to identify the CSF in a key market segment. He identified four as shown below. However, one is not really a CSF. Which one is not?
   a) On-time delivery.
   b) Level of customer service.
   c) Level of company advertising.
   d) Up-to-date design.

7. Three of the following criteria are relevant to market segmentation. Which one is not?
   a) Who the customers are.
   b) What customers buy.
   c) Why they buy.
   d) The price you charge.
8. Pareto's Law is often found to operate when

marketing data is analysed. If a company had a customer base of 200, how many of these are likely to account for approx. 80 per cent of the sales revenue? Is it:

a) 10? c) 38?
b) 22? d) 54?

9. A company analysed its three major competitors using CSFs and weightings gathered from research. It assessed each one as shown below. Which is the most dangerous competitor? What does it score?

Competitor Assessment Scores				
on a scale of 1–10 (high)				
CSF	Weighting	A	B	C
On-time delivery	0.5	9	5	7
Product quality	0.3	5	5	7
Quality of sales staff	0.2	4	8	4

10. Four companies operate in the same industrial market segment. Company A has a 10 per cent share of the market and operates with the lowest prices. Company B has a 6 per cent share and charges the highest prices. Company C has a 18 per cent share and has the most up-to-date facilities. Company D has a 12 per cent market share and the largest sales force. Which company is likely to be the most profitable?

a) Company A. c) Company C.
b) Company B. d) Company D.

Answers

Question 1

Product class	Beer	Cars	Vacuum cleaners	Cosmetics
Product sub-class	Bitter	4-wheel-drive	Upright vacuum cleaners	Lipstick
Product brand	Bass	Subaru	Hoover	Revlon

Question 2   The product range is designed to meet the needs of a market segment, not to define it.
Answer = a).

Question 3

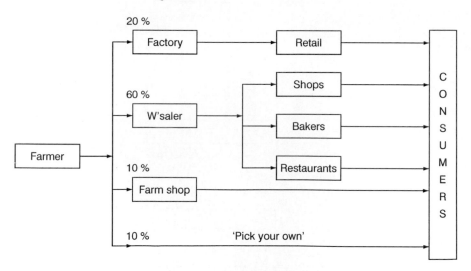

Question 4   Answer i) = D, ii) = A, iii) = B, iv) = E, v) = D, vi) = C1, vii) = C2, viii)= C1, ix) = B, x) = A.

Question 5   A differential benefit gives you a competitive advantage.
Answer = c).

Question 6   While the level of advertising may
impact on sales revenue, when seen
from the customer's point of view it
does not compare with factors   such as
delivery, service, design, etc.
Answer = c).

Question 7   Price is part of the marketing mix, and
may be irrelevant.
Answer = d).

Question 8   Pareto's law is also known as the 80/20
law, so 80 per cent of sales revenue can
be expected from roughly 20 per cent of
customers. 20 per cent of 200 is 40, thus
38 is the closest figure.
Answer = c).

Question 9   Note: All raw scores (1–10) are multi-
plied by the appropriate weighting factors and the results for each company
are totalled.
Answer = A.

Question 10 Note: This answer is based on the outcome of PIMS research, which indicates
that a company's profitability is
directly proportional to its market
share. Since all companies operate in
the same market segment, market
share must also be a relative measure of
satisfying customers.
Answer = c).

5

Understanding products and services prior to planning

The other half of the marketing audit, having considered whom we sell to, is what we sell to them. The central role that a product (here meaning product or service) plays in marketing management makes it such an important subject that mismanagement in this area is unlikely to be compensated for by good management in other areas. Understanding products by means of a product audit is a prerequisite to setting meaningful marketing objectives.

A product is the total experience of the customer or consumer when dealing with an organization. The discussion on market segmentation in Chapter 4 explained how a product is a problem solver, in the sense that it solves a customer's problems, and is also the means by which the company achieves its objectives. When a customer buys a product, he or she buys a particular bundle of benefits perceived as satisfying his or her own particular needs and wants.

As illustrated in Figure 5.1, a product or service can be envisaged as a set of concentric circles. Functional features (such as components and performance) form the core. This is encircled by added values that enhance the basic features (such as reputation, corporate image, and style of service and support), which is known as the product or service surround. Generally speaking, the product surround accounts for 80 per cent of a product's impact, while accounting for only 20 per cent of costs. The reverse tends to be true for the core product. The importance attributed to the intangible elements, specifically brand name and value perceptions, is worth special consideration.

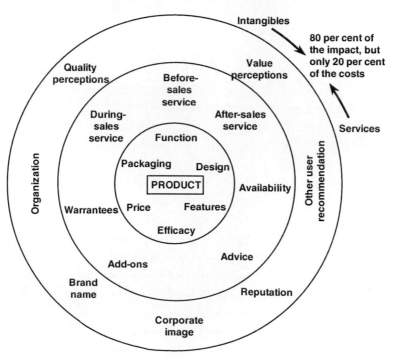

Figure 5.1   What is a product?

Where a relationship with the customer develops, this is often personified either by the company's name or by the brand name on the product itself. A brand is a name or symbol that identifies a product. The three principal components of a brand are: brand strategy (which stems from its position in the portfolio), brand positioning (what the brand actually does and what it competes with) and brand personality (its sensual, rational and emotional appeal). A successful brand identifies a product as having sustainable advantage. The reason why brands may be valued at figures far in excess of their balance sheet value is that it is relationships with customers, not factories, that generate profits, and it is company and brand names that secure these relationships. When brand names are neglected their distinctive values are eroded and they can no longer command a premium price. Consequently, they offer no unique added values and decay into commodities. Commodity markets are typically characterized by the lack of perceived differentiation by customers between competing offerings, and thus purchase decisions tend to be taken on the basis of price or availability and not on the brand or company name. Understanding the implications of brand value is fundamental to good marketing planning.

Branding: strategy, positioning and personality

Commodities are perceived to have no differentiation by customers leading to purchasing decisions on the basis of price

Having considered the vital factor of benefits as part of product management, we must ask ourselves whether one product is enough. Historians of technology have observed that all technical functions grow exponentially until they come up against some natural limiting factor, which causes them to slow down and eventually to decline as one technology is replaced by another. The same phenomenon applies to products, and is embodied in the product life

**Product life cycle –
Figure 5.2**

cycle (PLC), which plots the volume or value of sales of a product within a market or segment. From a management perspective, the PLC concept is helpful in that it focuses attention on the likely future sales pattern if no corrective action is taken. It is important to note that an organization is only concerned with the life cycle trend of a total market, or segment and with the sales of their product within it.

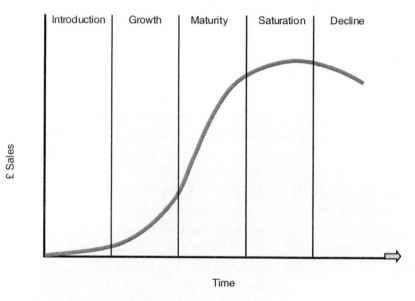

Figure 5.2 The product/market life cycle

**Diffusion of innovation –
Figure 5.3**

A useful extension of the PLC is what is termed 'diffusion of innovation'. Diffusion is the adoption of new products or services over time by consumers within social systems, as encouraged by marketing. It thus refers to the cumulative percentage of potential adopters of a new product or service over time. The actual rate of diffusion has been found to be a function of a product's:

● relative advantage (over existing products);

- compatibility (with lifestyles, values, etc);
- communicability (how easy it is to communicate);
- complexity;
- divisibility (whether it can it be tried out on a small scale before commitment).

Diffusion is also a function of the newness of the product itself, which can be classified broadly under three headings:

- continuous innovation (eg, the new miracle ingredient);
- dynamically continuous innovation (eg, disposable lighter);
- discontinuous innovation (eg, microwave oven).

Discovering a typology for those who are prepared to buy and try new products ('innovators' and 'early adopters') can seriously help in the promotion of new products. If we can target our early advertising and sales effort at winning over the trendsetters and opinion leaders in the market, then we can proactively increase our chances of also convincing the more conservative and sceptical customers to adopt our product.

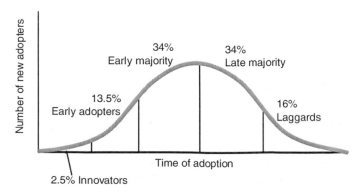

Figure 5.3   'Diffusion of innovation' curve

At any point in time, a review of an organization's different products would reveal different stages of growth, maturity and decline. If the objective is to grow in profitability over an extended period, then the product portfolio should reveal a situation in which new product introductions are timed so as to ensure continuous sales growth. The idea of a product portfolio is for an organization to meet its objectives by balancing sales growth, cash flow and risk. Ideally, a company should have a portfolio of products whose life cycles overlap. This guarantees continuity of income and growth potential. It is therefore essential that the whole portfolio is reviewed regularly and that an active policy towards new product development and divestment of old products is pursued.

All organizations have products that produce different levels of sales and profit margins. Profit occurs from the mix of products, ranging from low margin–high turnover to high margin–low turnover. The purpose of the marketing plan is to spell out at least three years in advance what the desired product combination is. RONA (return on net assets) can be portrayed as the business ratio:

$$\frac{\text{Net profit}}{\text{Net assets}} = \text{RONA}$$

Profits, however, are not always an appropriate indicator of portfolio performance as they will often reflect changes in the liquid assets of the company, such as inventories, capital equipment, or receivables, and thus do not indicate the true scope for future development. Cash flow, on the other hand, is a key determinant of a company's ability to develop its product portfolio.

The Boston Matrix, shown in Figure 5.4, is useful in product portfolio planning as it classifies a firm's products according to their cash usage and their cash generation along the two dimensions, relative market growth rate and market share. It shows graphically the positions of products in terms of relative market share and market growth, making it easier to see the relationship between multiple products. The Boston Matrix is based on the principle that cash – not profits – drive a product from one quadrant to another. It is a valuable planning tool for considering the implications of different product/market strategies and for formulating policies towards new product development, providing great care is taken over the 'market share' axis. The relationship of market share to cash generation is that the higher the market share, the higher the

The Boston Matrix

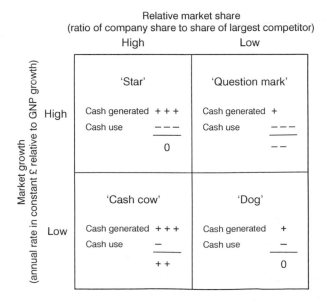

Figure 5.4   The Boston Matrix – cash management

output, and the lower the unit costs through economies of scale and the learning curve – thus a company can command higher margins and generate more revenue.

The four quadrants, or categories of products in the Boston Matrix are sometimes labelled 'star', 'cash cow', 'question mark' and 'dog' to indicate their respective prospects. The function of the Boston Matrix is to aid forward planning by suggesting strategy for the future development of the range: selectively invest in 'question marks'; invest in and grow 'stars'; maintain 'cash cows'; and critically examine 'dogs' and delete them as appropriate. 'Dog' products generate poor cash flow, and the costs of maintaining them can sometimes impede or destabilize overall business progress.

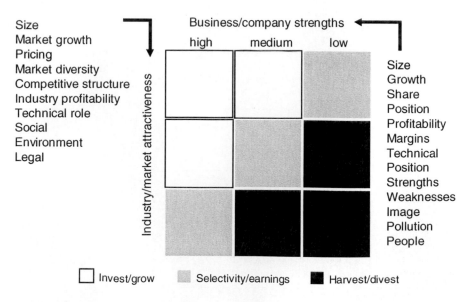

Figure 5.5 The directional policy matrix (DPM)

There are, however, factors other than market growth and market share that determine profitability, so many companies use an expanded version of this known as the directional policy matrix (DPM). As shown in Figure 5.5, the axes become relative business strengths and market attractiveness, indicating the relative importance of each market to the business. It is extremely important when using the DPM to define your markets clearly.

Directional policy matrix (DPM)

QUESTIONS AND ANSWERS

Questions

1. In what way should a marketer primarily view a product or service?
    a) In terms of its component parts and costs.
    b) In terms of its features and benefits.
    c) In terms of the total experience of the customer.
    d) In terms of its sales.

2. Below are some statements about products and services. Against each write T (true) or F (false).
    a) Services cost more overall than products. ( )
    b) Only a product can be consumed after it is produced. ( )
    c) The person delivering a service is part of the offer package. ( )
    d) Only products have features. ( )
    e) Only products can have a 'surround'. ( )
    f) It is difficult for services to be reproduced consistently. ( )

3. Which of the following are part of the core offer (C), or the product surround (S)?

a) packaging ( ) d) brand name ( )
b) customer   e) image   ( )
   service ( )   f) design   ( )
c) price ( )

4. One of the following statements about successful brands is not absolutely true. Please tick which one it is. A successful brand must:

a) Have a logo.
b) Be instantly recognizable.
c) Give a sustainable competitive advantage.
d) Deliver superior marketing performance.

5. For a product in the growth phase of its life cycle would you:

a) Let the growth trend develop naturally?
b) Find ways of cutting cost to maximize profit?
c) Spend to promote its competitiveness?
d) Reduce price to increase sales?

6. For a product at the saturation stage would you:

a) Increase promotion to extend its life?
b) Manage it for sustained earnings?
c) Kill it off to free resources for newer products?
d) Carry on as before and let nature take its course?

7. You are a late entrant into a market which, though it has peaked, is sizeable and attractive. What is your entry strategy?

a) Offer a keen price and stress the quality of your products.
b) Price high and stress the status that owner-ship brings.

   c) Price at mid-level and spend little on promotion.

   d) Price keenly and advertise heavily.

8. A company plotted a Boston Matrix for its products with the following results.

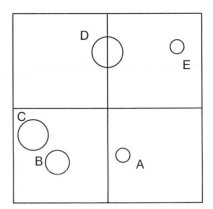

Which product ought to receive the major investment to ensure continued success? Tick your answer.

9. Which of the following could be market attractiveness factors (M), business strengths (B) or not significant (NS) in a domestic market?

   a) Few competitors. (   )

   b) High interest rates. (   )

   c) Customers requiring quality to ISO 9000. (   )

   d) Our location. (   )

   e) Non cyclical sales pattern. (   )

   f) State-of-the-art equipment. (   )

   g) Few barriers to entry. (   )

   h) Guaranteed supplies. (   )

10. The Boston Matrix is designed to be used for:
   a) Showing whether you have sufficient cash to run the business.
   b) Carrying out a competitive analysis.
   c) Demonstrating how products relate to markets.
   d) Showing areas of market growth.

Answers

Question 1   The customer pays for the total experience of a purchase.
Answer = c).

Question 2   Answer: a) = F, b) = T, c) = T, d) = F, e) = F, f) = T.

Question 3   Answer: a) = C, b) = S, c) = C, d) = S, e) = S, f) = C.

Question 4   All the others are essential features of brands.
Answer = a).

Question 5   It is important to promote products at their growth stage. They can be 'milked' later when they mature.
Answer = c).

Question 6   This also means minimizing promotion costs.
Answer = b).

Question 7   You have to appeal to the late majority and laggards in the market.
Answer = a).

Question 8   Answer: D = 2, but E would be acceptable. The reason is that the company has
no 'stars' and so one/some must be
acquired quickly to balance the portfolio.

Question 9   Answer: a) = M, b) = NS, c) = NS, d) = B,
e) = M, f) = B, g) = M, h) = B.
Note: For b) high interest rates will
affect all players in a domestic market
to the same extent, ie, level playing
field.
ISO 9000 operates similarly. To complete in a market you must meet its
quality standards, but once all players
are at this level there is no differential
advantage, ie business strengths.

Question 10 It shows at a glance how the product
portfolio is balanced.
Answer = a).

6

Setting marketing objectives and strategies

The setting of marketing objectives and strategies is the key step in the marketing planning process for it is the point at which all the information accumulated in the customer and market audit and product audit is translated into decisions about marketing direction and delivery.

MARKETING OBJECTIVES

Objectives are the core of managerial action, providing direction to the plans. An objective will ensure that a company knows what its strategies are expected to accomplish and when a particular strategy has accomplished its purpose. Without objectives, strategy decisions and all that follows will take place in a vacuum. The meaningfulness, and hence effectiveness, of any objective depends on the quality of information inputs and how closely it is related to and reflective of the organization's capabilities in the form of its assets, competences and reputation that have evolved over a number of years, or in the case of young companies, that have provided the basis for start up.

An objective contains three elements:

- the attribute chosen as a measure of efficiency, eg market share;
- the yardstick or scale by which the attribute is measured, eg operating period (by end of Year 3);
- the value on the scale which the organization seeks to attain, eg 25 per cent market share.

Marketing objectives: about products and markets

The important point about marketing objectives is that they are concerned solely with *products and markets*, for it is only by selling something to someone that the organization's financial goals can be achieved. If profits and cash flows are to be maximized, the organization must consider carefully how its current customer needs are changing and how its products/services offered need to change accordingly. Further, objectives should be measurable; otherwise they are not objectives. Marketing objectives are normally stated in standards of performance for a given operating period or conditions to be achieved by a given date. Thus measurement should be in terms of some or all of: sales volume, sales value, market share, profit, or percentage penetration of outlets. General terms such as 'maximize', 'minimize', 'penetrate' should be avoided unless quantification is included.

Marketing objectives consider the two main dimensions of commercial growth: product development and market development. The Ansoff matrix shown in

Figure 6.1 is a useful planning aid as it describes the four possible combinations of products and markets, or the four categories of marketing objectives:

● Selling existing products to existing markets/ segments (market penetration).

● Extending existing products to new markets/ segments (market extension).

● Developing new products for existing markets/ segments (product development).

● Developing new products for new markets/segments (diversification).

There will be different marketing responses to each permutation in the matrix, and the formulation of marketing objectives for each quadrant will be different for different companies. The term 'new products' infers a degree of technical innovation and 'new markets' assumes an element of unfamiliarity in a market situation. The newness factor of the product–market combination corresponds to the

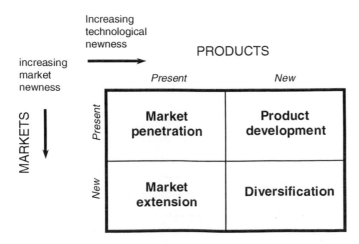

Figure 6.1 The Ansoff matrix

Ansoff Matrix: indication of levels of risk for a company

level of risk that the company has to manage. Thus pursuing marketing objectives concerned with new products in new markets is the riskiest strategy of all because it takes the organization furthest away from its known strengths and capabilities and further into the unknown. New resources and skills have to be developed. Diversification is what has led many companies to go bankrupt and why many of those that diversified through acquisition during periods of high economic growth have since divested themselves of businesses that were not basically compatible with their own distinctive competence.

The marketing objectives should be consistent with the information from the product life cycle analysis and portfolio matrix (or DPM, see Figure 5.5) discussed in Chapter 5. From the marketing audit and SWOT analysis, you will know: why customers want your products and services; which are your best markets and market segments; and the 'life' of your products or services. Most importantly, you will know from the portfolio matrix how the products/services in your range relate to each other in terms of raising funds. Creative and intelligent interpretation of the portfolio matrix is key to establishing the right marketing objectives for your company. Figure 6.2 is a list of guidelines for marketing and other functions, which should be considered *before* setting marketing objectives and strategies. The circles on the DPM, representing your sales in each market, can be moved to indicate their relative size and position in three years' time. You can do this to show first, where they will be if the company takes no action, and second, where you would ideally prefer them to be. These latter positions will become the marketing objectives.

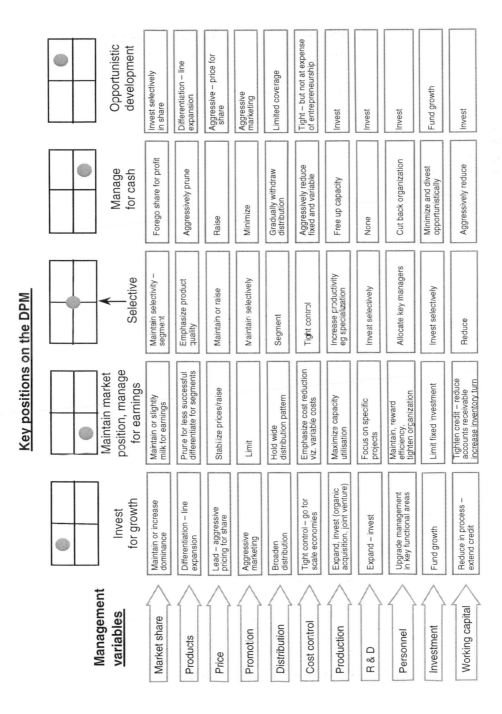

Key positions on the DPM

Management variables	Invest for growth	Maintain market position, manage for earnings	Selective	Manage for cash	Opportunistic development
Market share	Maintain or increase dominance	Maintain or slightly milk for earnings	Maintain selectivity – segment	Forego share for profit	Invest selectively in share
Products	Differentiation – line expansion	Prune for less successful differentiate for segments	Emphasize product quality	Aggressively prune	Differentiation – line expansion
Price	Lead – aggressive pricing for share	Stabilize prices/raise	Maintain or raise	Raise	Aggressive – price for share
Promotion	Aggressive marketing	Limit	Maintain selectively	Minimize	Aggressive marketing
Distribution	Broaden distribution	Hold wide distribution pattern	Segment	Gradually withdraw distribution	Limited coverage
Cost control	Tight control – go for scale economies	Emphasize cost reduction viz. variable costs	Tight control	Aggressively reduce fixed and variable	Tight – but not at expense of entrepreneurship
Production	Expand, invest (organic acquisition, joint venture)	Maximize capacity utilisation	Increase productivity eg specialization	Free up capacity	Invest
R & D	Expand – invest	Focus on specific projects	Invest selectively	None	Invest
Personnel	Upgrade management in key functional areas	Maintain, reward efficiency, tighten organization	Allocate key managers	Cut back organization	Invest
Investment	Fund growth	Limit fixed investment	Invest selectively	Minimize and divest opportunistically	Fund growth
Working capital	Reduce in process – extend credit	Tighten credit – reduce accounts receivable increase inventory turn	Reduce	Aggressively reduce	Invest

Figure 6.2 Plan guidelines for positioning on the DPM

As discussed in Chapter 2, corporate objectives lead to corporate strategies, which in turn suggest marketing objectives and strategies lower down the business hierarchy. Gap analysis is a technique used to explore the shortfall between the corporate objective and what can be achieved by various strategies. As described in Figure 6.3, what it says is that if the corporate sales and financial objectives are greater than the current long-range trends and forecasts, then there is a gap to be filled. The operations gap can be filled by reducing costs, improving the sales mix and/or increasing market share. The strategy gap can be filled by finding new user groups, entering new segments, geographical expansion, new product development, and/or diversification. The marketing audit should ensure that the method chosen to fill the gap is consistent with the company's capabilities and builds on its strengths.

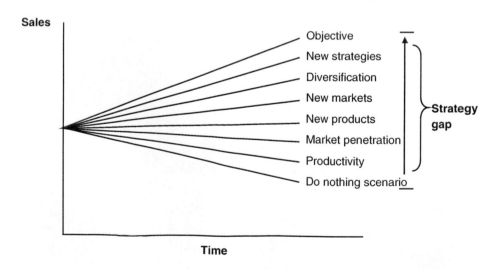

Figure 6.3 Gap analysis

MARKETING STRATEGIES

All organizations serve a mix of different types of market. Marketing strategy enables the organization to select the customers, and hence the markets, it wishes to deal with. It is the route by which the organization seeks to achieve its marketing objectives through the range of products/services it offers to its chosen markets. By indicating what strengths are to be developed, what weaknesses are to be remedied, and in what manner, marketing strategies enable operating decisions to bring the organization into the right relationship with the emerging pattern of market opportunities, which previous analysis has shown to offer the highest prospect of success.

Marketing strategies are generally concerned with the four 'P's of the marketing mix:

- Product – the general policies for product deletions, modifications, additions, design, branding, positioning, packaging, etc.
- Price – the general pricing policies to be followed for product groups in market segments.
- Place – the general policies for channels and customer service levels.
- Promotion – the general policies for communicating with customers under the relevant headings, such as advertising, sales force, sales promotion, public relations, exhibitions, direct mail, the internet, etc.

The main components of marketing strategy are: the company, customers, and competitors. When setting marketing strategies, it is important to know your position in the market, as well as the positions of your competitors, so that ideally you can meet customer needs by doing something your rivals aren't expecting and will find difficult to emulate or supersede. The point to remember about differentiation as a strategy is that you must still be cost-effective.

Porter's generic strategies

Michael Porter's generic strategies matrix, shown in Figure 6.4, demonstrates that some markets are inherently more prone to lack of differentiation in products and services. In such cases, the attainment of low costs must be a corporate goal if adequate margins are to be obtained. The ultimate strategy for commodity market situations, where there is no differentiation or cost advantage, is to move to either a cost leadership or niche strategy. A niche position is achieved through offering added value, whereas in a cost leadership position, the values offered are cost competitive.

Marketing strategies should state in broad terms *how* the marketing objectives are to be achieved. They should cover:

- the specific product policies (the range, technical specifications, additions, deletions, etc);
- the pricing policies to be followed for product groups in particular market segments;

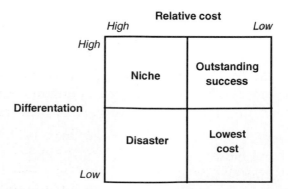

Figure 6.4 Porter's generic strategies matrix

- the customer service levels to be provided for specific market segments (such as maintenance support);
- the policies for communicating with customers under each of the main headings, such as sales force, advertising, sales promotion, etc, as appropriate.

Some of the marketing strategies available to managers include:

- change product design, performance, quality or features;
- change advertising or promotion;
- change unit price;
- change delivery or distribution;
- change service levels;
- improve marketing productivity (eg, improve sales mix);
- improve administrative productivity;
- consolidate product line;
- withdraw from markets;
- consolidate distribution;
- standardize design;
- acquire markets, products, facilities.

Marketing strategies define broadly the means of implementing the marketing plan and are not concerned with detailed courses of action, which are the one-year operational, or tactical plans derived from the strategic plans. However, those responsible for preparing strategic marketing plans will benefit from understanding the detail contained within operational plans for the main elements of the marketing mix. Therefore, let us consider next what should appear in the advertising and sales promotion plans, the sales plan, the pricing plan and the distribution plan (Chapters 7, 8, 9 and 10 respectively).

QUESTIONS AND ANSWERS

Questions

1. Using the Porter's 'generic strategies matrix' shown below, in which boxes would you place these businesses? Write the box letter in the brackets.

   i)   Cut price, no frills grocery store.   (   )
   ii) High price organic food store.   (   )
   iii) Successful supermarket with
        reputation for quality.   (   )
   iv) Traditional food store, stuck in the
        past.   (   )

2. The Acme Company have a corporate objective to generate 20 per cent return on capital employed in three years' time. To achieve this the company must then be earning £20 million in sales revenue. The marketing director calculates that a continuation of current strategies will only produce £15 million. Which of the following, taken individually will not help to close the gap?

a) Reduce discounts.

b) Develop new products.

c) Increase advertising.

d) Become more productive.

e) Cut costs.

f) Increase prices.

g) Develop new markets.

h) Improve the product mix.

i) Improve the customer mix.

j) Lower the revenue target.

3. There are five main strategies to apply to products according to their position on the directional policy matrix. What are they? Write your answers in the spaces provided.

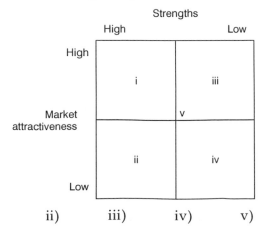

i)   ii)   iii)   iv)   v)

4. Which of the above would be best suited to:
   a) A 'cash cow'?   b) A 'star'?

5. Two opposing forces meet armed with muskets that take three minutes to reload. Force A has 100 soldiers and Force B, 200. However, the troops in Force A are better trained and can expect to bring down 20 per cent of their opponents in each volley. They are twice as effective as Force B.

   When either force is reduced to less than 50 per cent of its original number it will retire from the field.

   i) Assuming both fire the first volley simultaneously, who wins?
   a) Force A   b) Force B

   ii) Also, how long does this skirmish last if it is timed from the opening exchange?
   a) 6 minutes   c) 12 minutes
   b) 9 minutes   d) 15 minutes

6. The diversification box of the Ansoff matrix has to be treated with care because it represents:
   a) The least profitable options.
   b) The most risky options.
   c) The options which take longest to implement.
   d) The most costly options.

7. If you choose an invest strategy, which of the statements below are true (T) or false (F)?
   a) The market must be attractive.   (   )
   b) Sales volume must show a year-on-year increase.   (   )
   c) Prices should increase to cover costs.   (   )
   d) Marketing objectives should at best match market growth rates.   (   )

e) The market should be stable. ( )
f) The market should be growing. ( )

8. Which of the following are true (T) or false (F)?
To be successful, marketing strategies should ensure that:
   a) Prices cover costs on all
      products/services. ( )
   b) Quality is never less than the highest
      standard. ( )
   c) The sales force is the largest. ( )
   d) Changes in market needs are
      addressed. ( )

9. Gap analysis is used to:
   a) Monitor the gap between you and competitors.
   b) Identify gaps in your product range.
   c) Identify the shortfall from expected results if
      current strategies remain unchanged.
   d) Identify gaps in the SWOT analysis.

10. The Ansoff Matrix, shown below, helps to identify four broad strategies. These are:

i) New product   iii) Market
   development. (   )   extension.   (   )
ii) Market   iv) Diversification. (   )
   penetration.   (   )

Indicate which strategy fits in which box by
writing a, b, c or d in the brackets above.

Products

	Existing	New
Existing	a	b
New	d	c

Markets

Answers

Question 1   Answer: i) = d), ii) = a), iii) = b) and iv) =
              c).

Question 2   £5 million must be generated from new
              strategies. Increasing advertising, by
              itself will incur costs and not necessar-
              ily generate revenue. Cutting costs can
              influence profitability but will not gen-
              erate revenue. Lowering the target
              (moving the goalposts) is no way to run
              a business.
              Answer: c), e) and j).

Question 3   Answer: i) Invest for growth; ii) Maintain market position, manage for earnings; iii) Selective investment; iv) Manage for cash; v) Opportunistic development.

Question 4   Answer: a) = ii, Maintain; b) = i, Invest.

Question 5   After the opening exchange Force B is down to 160 men. The next round reduces it to 123, then 104, then approx. 80. Thus there are 3 loading periods after opening exchange = 9 minutes. Answer: i) = a), ii) =b).

Question 6   It doubles the risk by calling for new products and new markets. Answer = b).

Question 7   Answer: a) = T, b) = F, c) = F, d) = T, e) = F, f) = T.

Question 8   a) is false because it might be a suitable strategy to have a 'loss leader'.
b) is false – the customer is the arbiter of quality – the highest possible standard is not always required or possible.
c) is false because the quality of the salesforce is more important than its size.
Answer: a), b) and c) = F; d) =T.

Question 9   Answer = c).

Question 10 Answer: i) = b), ii) = a), iii) = d), iv) = c).

7

Advertising and sales promotion strategies

In order to achieve its marketing objectives, an organization has to communicate with both existing and potential customers. It can do so in a variety of ways, either on an impersonal or personal basis. Impersonal communication is accomplished indirectly, using advertising, promotion, point-of-sale displays, and public relations, while personal communication is undertaken directly, in face-to-face meetings, generally using a sales force. The armoury of communication techniques at the organization's disposal, which might be used singly or in combination, can be blended together into an effective and persuasive communications mix. The choice of communications mix should be the most cost-effective solution for achieving the organization's communications objectives that derived from its marketing objectives, which in turn originated from its corporate objectives.

Communications mix

The communications plan is the blueprint for integrating the various components of the communications mix. It comprises the advertising, sales promotion and sales plans. The former two involve impersonal communication, while the latter concerns personal communication. This chapter considers the *advertising plan* and the *sales promotion plan*. The sales plan is the focus of Chapter 8.

ADVERTISING STRATEGIES

Advertising (often referred to as 'above-the-line expenditure') uses measured media such as television, cinema, radio, print and electronic media (eg, banner advertising on web sites). The usual assumption is that advertising is deployed in an aggressive role and that all that changes over time is the creative content. But the role of advertising usually alters during the life cycle of a product. For example, the process of persuasion (awareness, interest, attitude formation, decision to act) cannot normally start until there is some level of awareness about a product or service in the marketplace. Creating awareness is therefore one of the most important objectives early on the PLC. If the offer has been correctly matched with customer needs and is perceived to be superior to competitors' offers, through the astute use of such vehicles as branding, pricing or customer-convenient distribution, then the customer will be persuaded to buy.

The 'diffusion of innovation' curve discussed in Chapter 5 is relevant here. Experience indicates that once the first 3 per cent of innovators have adopted the product, the early adopters will likely try it, and once the 8–10 per cent point is reached, the rest will likely follow suit. This pattern demonstrates the need for different kinds of advertising for each category of customer, and thus different sets of advertising objectives and strategies for different stages in a product's life cycle. It is worth remembering too that, for optimum effect, advertising effort can be directed not only at consumers, but at all those who influence commercial success, including channels, shareholders, media, employees, suppliers and government.

The first step in preparing an advertising plan is to decide on reasonable, achievable objectives for advertising. The acid test for confirming whether an objective is suitable as an advertising objective is to ask: 'Is it possible to achieve this objective by advertising alone?' If the answer is *no*, then it is not an objective for advertising.

A common misconception is that advertising objectives should be set in terms of sales increases. As advertising is one of a host of determinants of sales levels (which also includes product quality, price and customer service, for example), sales increases cannot be a direct objective of advertising. It is also important to be clear on the distinction between marketing objectives and advertising objectives. Marketing objectives are concerned with what products go to which markets, whereas advertising objectives are measurable targets concerned principally with changing attitudes and creating awareness.

Advertising objectives – about changing attitudes and creating awareness

There are two basic questions that advertising objectives should address: 'Who are the people we are trying to influence?' and 'What specific benefits or information are we trying to communicate to them?' Many companies use outside agencies to design their advertising. Advertising objectives, however, should *always* be set by you and *not* by an advertising agency.

There are many possible advertising objectives, such as:

- to convey information;
- to alter perceptions;
- to alter attitudes;
- to create desires;
- to establish connections, (eg, association of bacon and egg);
- to direct actions;
- to provide reassurance;
- to remind;
- to give reasons for buying;
- to demonstrate;
- to generate enquiries.

Having defined and agreed the advertising objectives, all other steps in the process of assembling the advertising strategy flow naturally from them. These subsequent steps address the following questions:

- Who?
  - Who are the target audience(s)?
  - What do they already know, feel, believe about us and our product/service?
  - What do they know, feel, believe about the competition?
  - What sort of people are they? How do we describe/identify them?
- What?
  - What response do we wish to evoke from the

target audience(s)? Are these specific communications *objectives*?

- What do we want to 'say', make them 'feel', 'believe', 'understand', 'know', about buying/using our product/service?
- What are we offering?
- What do we *not* want to convey?
- What are the priorities of importance for our objectives?
- What are there objectives which are *written* down and *agreed* by the company and advertising agency?

● How?

- How are our objectives to be embodied in an appealing form? What is our creative strategy/platform?
- What evidence do we have that this is acceptable and appropriate to our audience(s)?

● Where?

- Where is/are the most cost-effective place(s) to expose our communications (in cost terms vis-à-vis our audience)?
- Where is/are the most beneficial place(s) for our communications (in expected response terms vis-à-vis the 'quality' of the channels available)?

● When?

- When are our communications to be displayed/conveyed to our audience?
- What is the reasoning for our scheduling of advertisements/communications over time?
- What constraints limit our freedom of choice?

- - Do we have to fit in with other promotional activity on:
    - - other products/services supplied by our company?
    - - competitors' products/services?
    - - seasonal trends?
    - - special events in the market?
- The results:
  - - What results do we expect?
  - - How will we measure results?
  - - Do we intend to measure results and, if so, do we need to do anything *beforehand*?
  - - If we cannot say how we would measure precise results, then maybe our objectives are not sufficiently specific or are not communications objectives.
  - - How are we going to judge the relative success of our communications activities (good/bad/indifferent)?
  - - Should we have action standards?
- The budget:
  - - How much money do the intended activities need?
  - - How much money is going to be made available?
  - - How are we going to control expenditure?
- The schedule:
  - - Who is to do what and when?
  - - What is being spent on what, where and when?

SALES PROMOTION STRATEGIES

Sales promotion (often referred to as 'below-the-line expenditure') is non-face-to-face activity concerned with the promotion of sales. It is essentially a problem-solving activity designed to encourage customers to behave more in line with the economic interests of the company, ie to bring forward their decision to buy. Sales promotion involves the making of a featured offer to defined customers within a specific time limit. The offer must include benefits not inherent in the product or service, as opposed to the intangible benefits offered in advertising, such as adding value through appeals to imagery.

Sales promotion: encouraging a purchase

Typical tasks for sales promotion include: controlling stock movement; counteracting competitive activity; encouraging repeat purchase; securing marginal buyers; getting bills paid on time; and inducing trial purchase. It is generally used as a short-term, tactical initiative, in contrast with the notion of advertising as a long-term, strategic activity that changes with the PLC. However, sales promotion does have a strategic role to play in helping to strengthen the bond between seller and buyer, and thus a sales promotion strategy is required to ensure that each promotion increases the effectiveness of the next in terms of impact and investment of resources. Further, it is possible to establish a style of sales promotion that, if consistently applied, will help to establish the objectives of a product over a long period of time, which are flexible and have staying power.

Confusion about what sales promotion is, often results in expenditures not being properly recorded.

Sales promotion expenditure is sometimes considered, for example, as advertising or sales force expenditure, or as a general marketing expense, while loss of revenue from special price reductions is often not recorded at all. Not surprisingly, sales promotion is notoriously one of the most mismanaged of all marketing functions. In order to manage sales promotion expenditure effectively, it is essential that objectives for sales promotion be established, in the same way that objectives are developed for advertising, pricing or distribution. These will be dependent on the company's marketing objectives and may relate to any of the four 'P's.

Sales promotion seeks to influence:

Salespeople to sell
Customers to buy
Customers to use
Users to buy   more, earlier, faster,
Users to use   etc.
Distributors to stock

In order to achieve these objectives, the promotion can take one of three forms. It can involve:

- money (price reductions, coupons, competitions);
- goods (free goods, eg, two for the price of one, trade-ins, free trials, redeemable coupons, etc);
- services (guarantees, training, prizes for events, free services, etc).

When determining the nature of the sales promotion, you should decide first, which target group(s) need to be influenced most to make an impact on your sales problem and second, what type of promotion will have maximum appeal to that group. When considering the cost element, you must remember that the promotional costs have to be weighed up against the benefits of reducing the sales problem, which the sales promotion is intended to solve. The cost-effectiveness of the sales promotion must be established and integrated into the overall marketing plan.

The objectives for each sales promotion should be clearly stated, such as trial, repeat purchase, distribution, a shift in buying peaks, combating competition, and so on. Then the strategy to implement the objectives must be worked out. Sales promotion strategy should follow the standard route of: select the appropriate sales promotion technique; pretest; mount the promotion; and finally, evaluate in depth. Spending must be analysed and categorized by type of activity (eg, special packaging, special point-of-sale material, loss of revenue through price reductions, and so forth).

As for the sales promotion plan itself, the objectives, strategy and brief details of timing and costs should be included. It is important that the sales promotion plan should not be too detailed, and only an outline of it should appear in the marketing plan. (Detailed promotional instructions will follow as the marketing plan unfurls.) It is also important to ensure that any sales promotion is well coordinated in terms of what happens before, during and after the promotion. At different stages, different people might be participating and special resources might be required. Therefore the plan needs to be prepared in a simple way that most people can follow. As a guide, a sales promotion plan should contain the following:

Sales promotion: plan for activities before, during and after the promotion

Heading	Content
Introduction	Briefly summarize the problem upon which the promotion is designed to make an impact.
Objectives	Show how the objectives of the promotion are consistent with the marketing objectives.
Background	Provide the relevant data or justification for the promotion.
Promotional offer	Briefly, but precisely, provide details of the offer.
Eligibility	State who is eligible and where.
Timing	Specify when the offer is available (giving opening and closing dates).
Date plan	Give the dates and responsibilities for all elements of promotion.
Support	Identify special materials, samples, etc that are required by the sales force, retailers, etc.
Administration	Include budgets, storage, invoicing, delivery, etc.
Sales plan	Cover briefing meetings, targets, incentives, etc.
Sales presentation	List points to be covered.
Sales reporting	Give details of any special information required.
Assessment	Define how the promotion will be evaluated.

QUESTIONS AND ANSWERS

Questions

1. Which of the following are impersonal communications (I) and which are personal communications (P).

   a) advertising ( ) d) sales
   b) point of sale   promotion ( )
      display ( )   e) targeted mail ( )
   c) customer   f) salesperson
      help line ( )   visit ( )

2. Below is a matrix which illustrates the combinations of relationship between product/service complexity and its commercial uncertainty. Each box suggests that the buying process might be organized differently. Your task is to match the suggestions below with the appropriate boxes in the matrix. There is one mark for each correct answer.

   i) Routine buying process operated at
      a low management level. ( )
   ii) Buying decision made by top
      management. ( )

iii) Buying decision mainly delegated to
a technical specialist.   (   )
iv) Decision to buy referred to top
management for approval.   (   )

3. What is a benefit?
a) Something the customer wants.
b) Something cheaper than the competition.
c) Something the product supplies that the customer wants.
d) Something the product does better than its
competitors.

4. Tick which of the following communication
tasks lend themselves to impersonal
methods.
a) To announce a new service.
b) To show how a complex product can adapt to
specific situations.
c) To overcome objections.
d) To provide customer confidence.
e) To explain differential benefits.
f) To close a sale.

5. Part 1
What are the two missing group names in the
'diffusion of innovation' sequence shown below?

Innovators......Early majority......Late majority......

Part 2
What proportion of the total population,
approximately, does each of the missing groups
represent?

                    (   )   (   )

6. An advertisement is most effective if:
   a) It appears almost everywhere.
   b) It carries a single, believable message.
   c) It is very cleverly worded.
   d) It contains humour.

7. In the Boston Matrix, which box contains the products most likely to benefit from advertising?
   a) 'problem child'
   b) 'star'
   c) 'cash cow'
   d) 'dog'

8. Which of the following criteria would you use to measure the efficacy of an advertising campaign?
   a) An increase in sales revenue.
   b) The number of new customers.
   c) The extent to which the campaign met its objectives.
   d) The cost of winning each new customer or sale.

9. Decide which of the following statements about sales promotions are true (T) or false (F).
   a) The only legitimate target for a sales promotion is the customer. (   )
   b) Because a sales promotion is a 'below the line' activity it requires less planning. (   )
   c) Sales promotions are only a tactical marketing weapon. (   )
   d) Sales promotions can only be used with consumer goods. (   )
   e) The key to success with a sales promotion is always to have a new 'gimmick'. (   )

10. A Marketing Manager is considering running a '2 for the price of 1' sales promotion. Which of the reasons listed below would NOT justify this type of promotion?
   a) To boost falling profits.
   b) To shift slow moving products.
   c) To defend market share.
   d) To counter a competitor's new product launch.

Answers

Question 1   Answer: a) = I, b) = I, c) = P, d) = I, e) = P, f) = P.

Question 2   Answer: i) = d), ii) = a), iii) = c), iv) = b).

Question 3   Remember, a benefit is something bestowed by the product or service that the customer values. A cheaper price is not therefore a benefit if the customer seeks high quality or exclusivity. Nor is something the product does better a benefit, unless we can be sure that this particular advantage is what the customer seeks.
Answer = c).

Question 4   Answers: b), c) and f) can only be completed satisfactorily using face-to-face communication.
Answer: a), d) and e).

Question 5   Part 1: Answer: Early adopters (sometimes called opinion leaders) and laggards.
Part 2: Answer: 13.5 per cent and 16 per cent respectively.

Question 6 Although a) may sound attractive, the cost of such widespread exposure does not automatically guarantee success. It might only mean that an ineffective advertisement is seen by more people. With c) and d) the 'cleverness' may obscure the key message.
Answer = b).

Question 7 Promotional investment in 'stars' adds to their potential as 'cash cows' later in their life, and competition will be keen.
Answer = b).

Question 8 Advertising objectives can be many and varied. For example, some objectives may be to improve customer confidence or create an awareness of a new product. Thus the only correct answer is c).

Question 9 Answer: All are false.
a) This is patently untrue because intermediaries or your own salesforce could be the target for a sales promotion.
b) All promotions need careful planning.
c) Sales promotions can be used strategically, eg to defend market share, entice new customers, etc.
d) Promotions can work equally well with services.
e) A 'gimmick' might help, but the key to success is to provide an offer that

is attractive and thus motivates the target audience to take action.

Question 10 This type of promotion will do nothing for falling profits, but could be very successful in terms of meeting the other objectives.

Answer = a).

8

Sales strategies

While it is quite possible that some companies will not use advertising and sales promotion, very few fail to have some element of face-to-face selling in their marketing mix. Traditionally, companies had sales forces long before marketing was in vogue. This sometimes explains why, in many organizations, sales and marketing are regarded as two separate functions. However, where sales departments act independently of marketing, they often attain their short-term sales goals but fail to achieve the mix of products and markets consistent with its longer-term strategic marketing objectives.

Where sales act independently of marketing longer-term strategies often fail

Personal selling, or promotion via person-to-person conversation (be it at the customer's premises, by telephone, or elsewhere), is a vital part of the marketing mix. It offers the advantages of two-way communication, which advertising and sales promotion cannot provide. Sales messages can be made more customer-specific, questions can be asked and answered, and the salesperson can ask for an order and perhaps negotiate on price, delivery or special requirements. Such flexibility and personalization in communication can greatly enhance service levels and help close sales, but at a high cost. When the total costs of recruiting, managing and providing salespersons with all the necessary resources and support systems is considered, personal selling often accounts for more expenditure than advertising and sales promotion combined. It is therefore important to plan how personal selling will be integrated into the 'communications mix', and then to organize the logistics to ensure that the right results are achieved cost-effectively.

Personal selling provides two way communications – at a cost

Before attempting to produce a sales strategy, it is necessary to establish what information customers will require from the sales force. Communication efficiency depends on achieving a match between the information required and the information given. The organization must therefore identify the major influencers in each purchase decision and find out what information customers are likely to need at different stages of the buying process. It will also need to know if the customer is buying for the first time or contemplating a repeat order. Customer information needs may range from details about the product range and product performance, to price, running costs, guarantees, load sizes, competitor products, special offers, reordering, and so on.

The role of the salesperson is clearly about much more than just 'selling' and will vary according to the business concerned. A salesperson may be an order-taker, a negotiator, a demonstrator, or a composite of these and other roles. To optimize the sales force and obtain best value for money from personal selling, an organization must resolve three basic issues. It must determine the requisite number of salespeople, their precise sales role and how they are to be managed.

Salespeople essentially undertake three activities. They make calls, travel and administrate. By analysing their current workload and considering alternative ways of undertaking these responsibilities, the organization can decide what constitutes a reasonable workload (ie, how many calls it is possible to make in a working day given the concomitant time values for clerical tasks and travel) and how territories can be equitably allocated. Equally, an assessment of existing and potential customers should be made and the annual total number of calls calculated, bearing in mind that different customer categories need different call rates. The following formula is helpful in ascertaining how many salespeople are needed:

Sizing your sales force

$$\text{Number of salespeople} = \frac{\text{Annual total calls required}}{\text{Annual number of working days} \times \text{all salespeoples' calls per day}}$$

Having decided what role the sales force is to play in the communications mix per market segment, the next step is to draw up quantifiable objectives for them, including:

Sales objectives

- how much to sell (volume);
- what to sell (product/service mix);
- where to sell (market segments);
- allowable costs;
- profit margins.

The first three types of objectives derive directly from the marketing objectives and constitute the principal components of the sales strategy. The sales plan is, in effect, a translation of these figures/products/customers into individual targets for each sales representative, taking into account special factors such as their territory size, the size of customers within a particular territory, and so forth. Additional quantitative objectives might include the number of telephone contacts, service calls, distance travelled or reports submitted for a defined period.

Qualitative objectives should also be set. These will be related to the salesperson's skills in performing the job and can be appraised in terms of agreed standards of performance. The emphasis should be placed on measurable performance standards, such as expectations of work quality, efficiency, style and behaviour, rather than non-measurable factors, such as creativity, loyalty, interest and enthusiasm, which can easily be misconstrued as favouritism or unfairness.

Sales management – a very different role to selling

The key management activities involved in managing the sales force are summarized as:

- setting performance standards (both quantifiable and qualitative);
- monitoring achievements;
- helping/training those who are falling behind;
- setting the right motivational climate.

While monitoring what salespeople do can largely be accomplished through reports, sales figures and so on, assessing *how* they do things usually requires observing them in action. As a rule, the higher the uncertainty surrounding the salesperson, the territory, the product range, the customer, and so forth, the more frequently performance should be monitored. Having measurable standards of performance enables managers to identify the area and nature of help that salesperson needs, and to respond appropriately. For instance, he or she may need more information about prices and products, more support in terms of administration or joint visits, or more training to improve his or her skills set.

Perhaps most crucial of all is creating the right motivational climate. To maximize sales force performance it is necessary to achieve the optimal balance between incentives and disincentives. While remuneration will always be a key determinant of motivation, sales managers can improve sales force performance by clarifying performance expectations, providing rewards consistent with performance, giving due praise and recognition, ensuring freedom from fear and worry, and encouraging in their sales team a sense of doing a job that is worthwhile and valued.

Due to the uniqueness of each business situation and sales force make-up, no two sales plans will be exactly the same. However, some general guidelines can be given. Table 8.1 is an example of setting objectives for an individual salesperson. These objectives will be the logical result of breaking down the marketing objectives into actual sales targets.

Table 8.1 Objectives for the individual salesperson (based on the original work of Stephen P Morse when at Urwick Orr and Partners)

Task	The standard	How to set the standard	How to measure performance	What to look for
1 To achieve personal sales targets	Sales target per period of time for individual groups and/or products	Analysis of • territory potential • individual customers' potential. Discussion and agreement between salesperson and manager	Comparison of individual salesperson's product sales against targets	Significant shortfall between target and achievement over a meaningful period
2 To sell the required range and quantity to individual customers	Achievement of specified range and quantity of sales to a particular customer or group of customers within an agreed time period	Analysis of individual customer records of • potential • present sales. Discussion and agreement between manager and salesperson	Scrutiny of individual customer records. Observation of selling in the field	Failure to achieve agreed objectives. Complacency with range of sales made to individual customers
3 To plan journeys and call frequencies to achieve the minimum practical selling cost	To achieve appropriate call frequency on individual customers. Number of live customer calls during a given time period	Analysis of individual customers' potential. Analysis of order/call ratios. Discussion and agreement between manager and salesperson	Scrutiny of individual customer records. Analysis of order/call ratio. Examination of call reports	High ratio of calls to an individual customer relative to that customer's yield. Shortfall on agreed total number of calls made over an agreed time period
4 To acquire new customers	Number of prospect calls during time period. Selling new products to existing customers	Identify total number of potential and actual customers who could produce results. Identify opportunity areas for prospecting	Examination of • call reports • records of new accounts opened • ratio of existing to potential customers	Shortfall in number of prospect calls from agreed standard. Low ratio of existing to potential customers
5 To make a sales approach of the required quality	To exercise the necessary skills and techniques required to achieve the identified objective of each element of the sales approach. Continuous use of sales material	Standard to be agreed in discussion between manager and salesperson related to company standards laid down	Regular observations of field selling using a systematic analysis of performance in each stage of the sales approach	Failure to • identify objective of each stage of sales approach • identify specific areas of skill, weakness • use of support material

QUESTIONS AND ANSWERS

Questions

1. Which of the following statements is true? Most companies:
    a) Spend more on advertising than on the sales force.
    b) Spend more on sales promotions than the sales force.
    c) Spend more on the sales force than advertising and sales promotion together.
    d) Spend about the same on each.

2. Which of these is true? The real secret to success in sales depends upon:
    a) Having up-to-date product knowledge.
    b) Understanding the customers' buying processes.
    c) Having equal sized sales territories.
    d) Having a good incentive scheme for sales staff.

3. Deciding how many salespeople you need can be critical. Should the decision be based upon:
    a) What you can afford?
    b) What your competitors have?
    c) The minimum practical selling cost?
    d) Enough to service customers as agreed in the marketing plan?

4. Which of the following are true (T) or false (F)? A good salesperson will:
    a) Make meetings a two-way conversation.   (   )

   b) Know that good products sell
      themselves.   (   )
   c) Be an extrovert.   (   )
   d) Customize his or her message for
      each meeting.   (   )
   e) Demonstrate vast product knowledge
      at every opportunity.   (   )
   f) Recognize buying signals quickly.   (   )

5. It was found that all of a company's customers
   could be positioned on the following matrix. If
   you were the sales manager, what order of priority would you give to the customer communications in each box?

Quality of relationship

Relative cost

	Poor	Good
High	A	B
Business potential		
Low	C	D

   a) Top priority   Box (   )
   b) Next   Box (   )
   c) Next   Box (   )
   d) Lowest priority   Box (   )

6. Tick in which of the following situations telephone selling could be used successfully.
   a) To deal with a reorder.
   b) To deal with distant customers.
   c) To deal with awkward customers.
   d) To deal with a product launch.

7. Which of the following is the most important? A good salesperson will be strong on:
   a) Striking up a friendship with the customer.
   b) Stressing the features of the product.
   c) Sticking to his or her preplanned presentation.
   d) Identifying the customer's problems.

8. Which of these is the most accurate statement? The customer's decision making unit (DMU) consists of:
   a) Those people who are involved in the choice of supplier.
   b) A representative of all organizational functions.
   c) The buyer, plus someone from the technical and finance departments.
   d) The buyer and the CEO.

9. Choose the most appropriate ending for the following statement. 'The key role for a sales manager is …'
   a) To be available at all times to deal with problems experienced by customers or the sales force.
   b) To develop sales representatives.
   c) To negotiate prices with major customers.
   d) To ensure that all sales reports are submitted on time and that sales staff do not abuse their expenses.

10. A key business ratio is:

$$\frac{\text{Net Profit}}{\text{Net Assets}} = \text{RONA}$$

This is calculated by using this formula:

$$\frac{\text{Net Profit}}{Y} \times \frac{Y}{\text{Net Assets}}$$

What is Y? Is it:
a) Total assets?
b) Cost of sales?
c) Working capital, ie capital employed – fixed assets?
d) Sales revenue?

Answers

Question 1   Several pieces of research support view c) UNLESS the company is in mail order or promotion-driven sales. Answer = c).

Question 2   Answer: a) and d) may have some bearing on sales success, but b) is the critical factor.

Question 3   Although some companies resort to a), b) and c), d) is the only sensible answer.

Question 4   Answer: T = a), d) and f). These all help the sales process. F = b), c) and e) which can derail it.

Question 5   Answer:
- a) = A. Improving relationships with high potential clients must be rated highly.
- b) = B. Maintaining good relationships with important customers is easier than making them in the first place.
- c) = D. Squeezing extra business out of those with whom the company has a good relationship comes next.
- d) = C. This is clearly the lowest priority; in fact, who wants this business?

Question 6   Answer: a) and b) – assuming the product was not too complex.

Question 7   Note: a failure to do this makes it impossible to meet the customers' needs.
Answer = d).

Question 8   This also explains why the composition of the DMU can vary from company to company and according to the nature of the purchase.
Answer = a).

Question 9   Like any other manager, the sales manager has to get results through others, not do their job for them. Thus developing each sales representative is a key task for successful managers.
Answer = b).

Question 10   Answer = d).

9

Price strategies

Pricing is a marketing 'tool' just as much as the communications devices of advertising, sales promotion and the use of the sales force. Moreover, it is generally easier and quicker to change a price than it is to alter an advertising campaign, revamp a sales promotion, or to deploy the sales force in a different manner. The pricing decision is important for two main reasons: price not only affects the margin through its impact on revenue; it also affects the quantity sold through its influence on demand. In short, price has an interactive effect on the other elements of the marketing mix, so it is essential that it is part of a conscious marketing scheme, with objectives that have been clearly defined.

The reason why pricing is rarely separated out and put into a plan of its own is because it is so integral to the offer that it is generally included as part of

> Price has an interactive effect on other elements of the marketing mix

Pricing and internal debate

the product/segment plans. Pricing is also tradition-ally a source of disagreement between marketers and accountants: the marketer sometimes wants to hold or reduce the net selling price in order to increase market share, while the accountant often wants to increase the price of a product in order to maximize profitability. Certainly, any team comprising a financially alert marketer and a marketing-orientated accountant will make formidable opposition in the marketplace.

When trying to resolve the question of whether the role of pricing should be to increase profitability or to increase market share, a number of factors should be considered:

- objectives (corporate and marketing) and the product portfolio;
- PLC (product life cycle);
- the product's position in the market;
- competitors;
- potential competitors;
- costs (your own and the competitors');
- channels of distribution.

We know that it is important for an organization to have a well-defined hierarchy of objectives to which all its activities and actions, including pricing, can be related. As corporate objectives will influence marketing objectives, so marketing objectives will influence pricing objectives. For instance, marketing objectives for a particular product may dictate a short-term emphasis on profitability rather than market share, which will obviously influence the pricing strategy. This will be a function of that product's position vis-à-vis other products in the portfolio. The setting of marketing objectives for any particular product, then, is the starting point in any consideration of pricing. The portfolio matrix discussed earlier in Chapters 5 and 6 indicates that prices should be selected as follows:

The links with marketing objectives and portfolio analysis

- 'question mark' – price competitively to get market share;
- 'star' – price to maintain/increase market share;
- 'cash cow' – stabilize or even raise price;
- 'dog' – raise price.

Any pricing policy should also reflect the fact that the role of pricing will change over a product's life cycle. The product's position on its life cycle will suggest the following pricing strategies:

The links with the product life cycle

- introduction – either price low to capture market share, or price high in recognition of novelty and prestige;
- growth – price low (competitively) to get market share;
- maturity – as per growth phase;
- saturation – stabilize price, consider raising it;
- decline – raise price.

In addition, the product's position in the marketplace should factor in the pricing decision. It would be foolish, for example, to position a product as a high-quality, exclusive item, and then to price it too low. Price is one of the clearest signals customers have of the value of the offer the company is making them, and there has to be a sensible relationship between the two.

Product positioning

Competitors' pricing strategies should thus be taken into account. This raises the issues of product

Differentiating your offer

positioning and market segmentation. Wherever possible, a company should be seeking to blend the ingredients of the marketing mix in such a way that their 'offer' to the customer cannot be compared to anyone else's 'offer'. For, if two products are perceived as the same, the one with the lowest price will win most of the time. It is therefore necessary to analyse the prices charged by your competitors for their versions of your product or service, before deciding your own price.

Potential competitors should be another consideration. Some firms launch new products at high prices to recover their investment costs, only to find that they have provided a price 'umbrella' to entice competitors, who then launch similar products at much lower prices, thus moving down the experience curve quicker, often taking the originating company's market away from it in the process. A lower launch price, with possibly a quicker rate of diffusion and hence a greater rate of experience, may make it more difficult for a potential competitor to enter the

Skimming and penetration strategies

market profitably. These scenarios represent 'skimming' and 'penetration' policies, respectively.

Costs should also figure in the pricing equation, both the company's own costs and those of its competitors. The most common way of setting price is to

Danger of cost-plus pricing

use the cost-plus approach, arriving at a price that yields margins commensurate with declared profit objectives. Whatever costing system is used as the basis for reaching pricing decisions, it must be accurate, for without this there is no point of reference to put pricing into perspective. Costing systems that allocate fixed costs to all products in the range can produce misleading results. Knowing what the customer is prepared to pay for your product/service (the going rate price), consider different costing options, with the objective of getting the average cost per unit as low as possible, thereby securing a wider range of options. Caution should be exercised to ensure as much as possible that the pricing strategy applied to one product does not adversely affect the pricing strategies used for other products in the range, and that all chosen pricing policies work collectively in support of the organization's overall strategic objectives.

Where channel intermediaries are used, such as wholesalers, distributors and retailers, the company will need to consider rewarding them for their services. This reward is in effect a payment for the services they provide and for the costs saved by the supplier. However, the total channel margin may have to be shared between several intermediaries and still reach the consumer at a competitive price. Various types of margins are commonly encountered, most of which take the form of discounts against a nominal price list. These are:

Pricing and channel intermediaries

- Trade discount. This is a discount given against the pricelist for services made available by the intermediary, eg, holding inventory, buying in bulk, redistribution, etc.

- Quantity discount. This is a discount given to intermediaries who order in large lots.

- Promotional discount. This is the discount given to distributors to encourage them to share jointly in the promotion of the product(s) involved.

- Cash discount. In order to encourage prompt payments of accounts, a cash discount of around 2.5 per cent for payment within 10 days is often offered.

Margin management can thus be viewed as a matter of trade-offs of cost versus the added value of using distributors, with the objective of achieving the organization's marketing goals. The question of margins (both the margin retained by the firm and thus by implication the margin allowed the distributor) should therefore be addressed in the context of overall marketing strategy and the financial policy and capital structure of the firm. As a general rule, the company should give away only the costs it saves by using an intermediary.

In summary, the pricing plan should consider all the factors affecting price, which comprise:

- marketing objectives;
- the cost structure;
- legal constraints;
- consumer attitudes;
- competition (direct);
- competition (substitutes);
- company / product image;
- economic situation.

QUESTIONS AND ANSWERS

Questions

1. It is often claimed that a 'cost plus' pricing policy can be dangerous. Is this because:
   a) It gives accountants too much power?
   b) It does not reflect the market?
   c) It is not very accurate?
   d) It is too difficult to apply?

2. Below is a typical demand curve. Referring to this, which of these statements is the most accurate?
   a) It is important to set price P2 at a level which ensures that production capacity is filled, Q2.
   b) It is important to maximize the price, P1, even if demand is limited to Q1.
   c) It is important to find whichever P x Q combination along the curve gives the best result for achieving an organization's objectives.

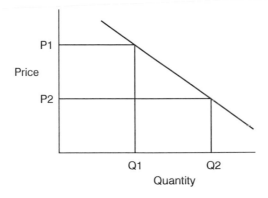

3. A company has a portfolio that contains five 'question marks'. What ought to be its pricing policy towards them?
   a) Should all be priced low in order to win market share?
   b) Should all be priced high to maximize revenue?
   c) Should only the best prospects be priced high?
   d) Should only the best prospects be priced low?

4. A popular form of positioning map is price ver-
    sus quality, shown below. Which of the zones A,
    B, C or D on the map correspond to the descrip-
    tions given here?

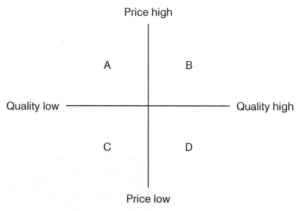

a) Lost profits.
b) Opportunistic, maybe unsustainable, pricing.

5. Successful pricing strategies are likely to result
    from examining which of the factors listed
    below? Tick your choice.
    a) The costs of production and what competi-
        tors are doing.
    b) Your objectives for market share, what the cus-
        tomer will pay, costs and competitors' prices.
    c) Your costs, current prices in the market and
        the experience curve.
    d) The experience curve, your raw material
        costs and competitors' prices.

6. The PIMS database shows that there is a distinct
    relationship between quality, sales, price, costs
    and market share. Which of the combinations
    below is correct, a, b, c or d?
    Note: I = increases, D = decreases.

	Market share	Sales price	Costs	Quality	Answer
a	I	D	I	I	
b	D	D	I	I	
c	I	D	I	D	
d	I	I	D	I	

7. Which of the following circumstances favours a skimming policy (S) and which ones a penetration policy (P)?
   a) Demand is likely to be price inelastic. ( )
   b) Little is known about the costs of producing and marketing the product. ( )
   c) Competitors are likely to enter the market quickly. ( )
   d) There are no distinct and separate price–market segments. ( )
   e) Demand is likely to be price elastic. ( )
   f) There are likely to be different price–market segments. ( )
   g) There is a high probability that big savings can be made in production and/or marketing costs with large sales volume. ( )
   h) Some competitors are expected to leave the market. ( )

8. In the context of the product life cycle, what would be your pricing policy for a product at its maturity phase? Would you:
   a) Price competitively? c) Stabilize prices?
   b) Price low? d) Raise prices?

9. A skimming policy may be best described as one where:
   a) Prices are set low to mop up all the price sensitive customers.
   b) Prices are set high to maximize sales margins.
   c) Prices are set just above average to attract the more discerning customers.
   d) Prices are allowed to fluctuate in line with market conditions.

10. What would be the objective of offering a distributor a cash discount?
    a) To encourage prompt payment.
    b) To encourage the volume of business generated by the distributor.
    c) To encourage a distributor to stock whole range of products.
    d) To encourage the distributor's promotional efforts.

Answers

Question 1 While a cynic might prefer a), the true answer is b).

Question 2 Answer = c).

Question 3 The company will only invest in the very best prospects and price these competitively to gain market share. Answer = d).

Question 4 Answer: a) = D. Here the company is supplying high quality but not asking the price commensurate with this.

Answer: b) = A. Here the company is charging a high price yet the product is of poor quality.

Question 5 Your pricing strategy must reflect your marketing objectives.
However, it will be tempered by a realistic assessment of what customers are prepared to pay, the margin you expect to make (hence the need to know costs) and the price of competing products or services.
Answer = b).

Question 6 Answer = d).

Question 7 Answer: Skimming policy = a), b), f) and h), for all of these situations suggest that price can be raised towards the top end of 'what the market will bear'. Penetration policy = c), d), e) and g), here are circumstances where pricing must be very competitive if you are to make impact.

Question 8 Answer = a). In all likelihood this is still a star (the market is probably still growing) and needs to be managed as one. Later, when demand (and competition) abates it can be appropriate to stabilize the price and minimize promotional costs.

Question 9 Answer = b) assuming of course that the market conditions are favourable for this strategy.

Question 10 Answer = a). Note, in order to make impact on volume of sales, some form of volume discount would be arranged. Similarly, other incentives (not necessarily cash) would reward the other specific distribution objectives, eg, prizes or services.

10

Place (distribution and customer service) strategies

For many businesses, distribution plays a small part in their marketing plans. When it is considered, the prime concern seems to focus on the physical aspects, the logistics of getting goods transported from the company to the customer. Distribution, however, embraces a much broader concept than just the delivery of goods. In addition, it takes into account the strategic importance of distribution channels and the potential value of channel intermediaries. It also ensures that 'customer service' is kept in the forefront of the company's deliberations about its marketing policies.

Supply chain management

Unless there is a formalized distribution structure, distribution-related activities may be spread across production, marketing, procurement, finance and so on, leading to conflicts of interest between distribution decisions. A more centralized, inter-related distribution system, often referred to as 'logistics' or 'the supply chain', will ensure that one distribution activity is traded off against another to arrive at the most efficient system overall. The person responsible for distribution, therefore, has several variables to contend with in the search for trade-offs; taken together these constitute the *distribution mix*. There are five components to manage in the physical distribution of tangible products:

- Facilities – the number, size and geographical location of storage and distribution depots.
- Inventory – the stockholding levels throughout the distribution chain consistent with customers' service expectations.
- Transport – the modes of transport, delivery schedules, etc.
- Communications – the flow of information, eg, order processing, invoicing, forecasting, etc.
- Unitization – the way in which goods are packaged and assembled into large units, eg, palletization, containerization, etc.

Together, these five areas make up the total cost of distribution within a company. In some businesses, distribution costs can amount to 20 per cent of the selling price. This emphasizes the importance of considering distribution within the context of the entire marketing mix.

The ultimate purpose of any distribution plan, and the fundamental role of a company's distribution function, is to ensure that the right product is in the right place at the right time. If a product is not available when and where the customer wants it, it will surely fail in the market. This implies the need for some organization of resources into channels through which the product or service can move from its original source of supply to its ultimate consumption. The optimal choice of distribution channels will be dependent on the type of business concerned and the markets it is engaged in. While some companies use multiple channels, often involving several intermediaries, others choose to deal with their customers more directly. There are basically three options from which to choose:

Channels to market

- to sell direct to the customer/user;
- to sell to customer/users through intermediaries;
- to use a combination of the two points above (ie, dual distribution).

The role of an intermediary is to provide the means of achieving the widest possible market coverage at lowest unit cost. The use of an intermediary carries benefits for the manufacturer, but it also involves significant 'costs', the most important of which is the loss of control that accompanies such a channel strategy. Marketing channel decisions therefore require a cost/benefit appraisal of the implications of all the physical distribution alternatives, taking into consideration marketing strategy, the appropriateness of the channel to the product, the integrity and compatibility of the channel partner and customer requirements, as well as the comparative costs of selling and distribution. It is also important to remember that the product's physical path may well be different from the one taken by the process of exchange of money for goods (or transfer of ownership), particularly as many intermediaries share in the financial risk with the supplier.

The output of an integrated distribution system is customer service. Customer service is a system organized to provide a continuing link between the first contact with the customer, through to the time the order is received and the goods/services delivered and used, with the objective of satisfying customer needs continuously. As customer service is increasingly a key determinant of competitive advantage, and it is likely that different customer segments will require different levels of customer service, managing customer service provision is a complex and critical activity.

A balance between service levels and cost

It is also an expensive one. Operating service levels at 100 per cent can be crippling to the supplier, yet to drop below an acceptable level is to surrender one's market share to a competitor. Research has shown that once the service level (defined as the percentage of occasions the product is available to customers, when and where they want it) increases beyond the 70–80 per cent mark, the associated costs increase exponentially. In many cases, such high levels of customer service are not necessary. Thus the choice of service level for a particular product should balance supplier costs and customer benefits; the point of balance being reached when the costs equal the extra revenue gained by the extra level of availability. Service level decisions will be tempered by other influential factors, such as:

- The contribution to fixed costs, eg can it bear the cost of an upgraded service level?
- The nature of the market, eg, are there substitute products?
- The nature of the competition, eg, do they offer better service levels?
- The nature of the distribution channel, eg, do we sell direct or through intermediaries?

The key to marketing success is to develop a customer service package (the customer's perception of supply chain performance) that embraces product availability, with attractive order cycle times and mechanisms for minimizing customer inconvenience arising from order cycle times. This necessitates a dynamic knowledge of both customer needs and preferences, and the company's ability to satisfy them. The proven direct correlation between customer retention and profitability suggests that the costs of providing enhanced customer service could be seen as a justified investment in customer retention.

As in the development of the other tactical plans, distribution planning should begin with the distribution audit (see Figure 2.1), from which distribution objectives and strategies can be established. Distribution objectives can be many and varied, but the following are considered basic for marketing purposes:

Distribution objectives

- objectives related to outlet penetration by type of distribution;
- objectives related to inventory range and levels to be held;
- objectives related to distributor sales and sales promotion activities;
- objectives related to other specific customer development programmes, eg, incentives for distributors.

A simple, iterative approach to distribution planning can be summarized as the following steps; the content of which will shape the distribution strategy.

1. Determine marketing objectives.
2. Evaluate changing conditions in distribution at all levels.

3. Determine the distribution task within overall marketing strategy.
4. Establish a distribution policy in terms of type, number and level of outlets to be used.
5. Set performance standards for distributors.
6. Obtain performance information.
7. Compare actual with anticipated performance.
8. Make improvements where necessary.

The interrelationship between developing the marketing plan and developing the distribution plan is usefully depicted in Figure 10.1.

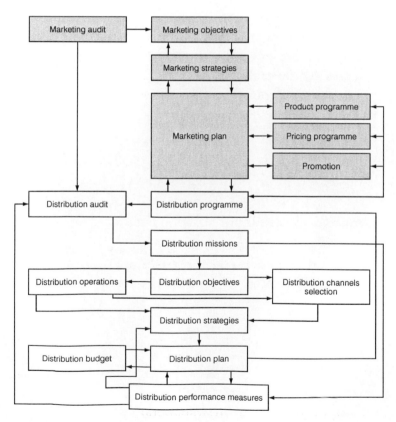

Figure 10.1 The distribution plan in relation to the marketing plan

QUESTIONS AND ANSWERS

Questions

1. Mark each of the following statements either true
    (T) or false (F).
    Distribution is only concerned with:
    a) The physical transportation of goods.   (   )
    b) Establishing the best channels for
        getting goods to customers.   (   )
    c) Optimizing the level of availability of
        goods for customers.   (   )

2. The distribution mix is made up of five items.
    Here are four of them. What is the missing item?
    Write your answer in the space provided.
    Facilities   Inventory   Transport   Unitization

    ....

3. Which of the following criteria would be attrac-
    tive when it comes to selecting a channel inter-
    mediary?
    a) Creditworthiness is unknown.
    b) The intermediary carries competitor's lines.
    c) Its management is enthusiastic and innovative.
    d) It is experienced in selling to our market.
    e) It has a very well trained sales team.
    f) It is close to a motorway.

4. Product availability levels are a key component of
    customer service. Which of the following would
    be most susceptible to stock-out situations?
    a) prescription drugs;   d) cars;
    b) household furniture;   e) newspapers;
    c) flowers;   f) fashion wear.

5. Complete the following sentence by placing a tick against the most appropriate endings(s) of those given below.

   For customer service to be successful it is important that...
   a) All customers are treated the same.
   b) Customers' expectations of service are met.
   c) Quality standards are maintained to the highest levels.
   d) There is a designated customer service manager.

6. Customer retention is very important for any business because primarily:
   a) It makes it easier for marketing planning.
   b) It increases profitability.
   c) It reduces the number of complaints received.

7. The customer service package ought to be centred around:
   a) Whatever customer complaints suggest.
   b) What you believe customers want.
   c) Whatever are the key determinants of customer satisfaction.
   d) Having a well-trained and polite staff.

8. A strawberry grower sells some of his crop at the local market, some to a wholesaler who supplies bakers and restaurants in the nearest large town, the rest goes to a jam factory and to 'pick your own' enthusiasts. Which of the following 'maps', showing how the fruit reaches the consumers is the correct representation of his business? Record your answer by ticking a, b or c. Please note that the names of intermediaries have been omitted, otherwise the question would be too simple.

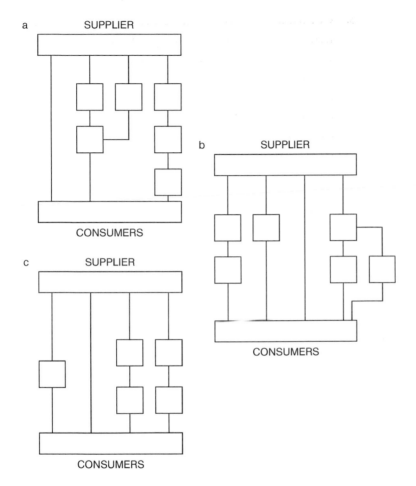

9. Which of the following distribution objectives can be considered as basic for marketing purposes?
   a) To hold an inventory range at specific levels.
   b) To replace vehicle fleet.
   c) To use approved carrier instead of own transport.
   d) To have an appropriate incentive scheme for distributors.
   e) To set outlet penetration levels per channel.
   f) To refurbish warehouses.

10. In seeking to become more competitive in a particular distribution channel, which of the following factors would most influence your thinking?
   a) Your relative strengths and weaknesses.
   b) The costs associated with operating in that channel.
   c) The number of competitors.
   d) The size of the market.

Answers

Question 1   Answer: All are false, because distribution is concerned with all three factors listed above. All must be considered by the marketer.

Question 2   Answer: Communications.

Question 3   Answer: Attractiveness features = c), d) and e). While f) may appear to be attractive, being near a motorway by itself is not enough. The distributor's location vis-à-vis the customers and ourselves is far more significant.

Question 4   Answer: a), c), e) and f) are usually required immediately, whereas people are prepared to select a model of car or furniture from a showroom and wait for it to be delivered at some later date.

Question 5   Answer = b)
            Note that (a) is not true because customers in different market segments will

be likely to require a different customer service 'package'. (c) is false because the highest possible standards could far exceed customer expectations and/or what competitors are offering, thus increasing costs unnecessarily. (d) is wrong because having good customer service is not dependent upon having a designated manager. Having a customer service policy and training staff to fulfil it are likely to be more important factors.

Question 6   While a) and c) may be partly true, the prime benefit of customer retention is its impact on profitability. Hence b) is the answer.
Answer = b).

Question 7   Note that while a) appears to be a reasonable answer, it could lead to customer service being focused on the wrong things. Similarly, staff training results from having the correct customer service objectives, not the other way round.
Answer = c).

Question 8   Answer = b).
Reading from left to right:
Line 1 = to jam factory to retailers to consumers
Line 2 = to market to consumers
Line 3 = to 'pick your own' – no intermediaries
Line 4 = to wholesaler, then through either bakers or restaurants

Question 9 Answer: a), d) and e), the others are merely means of reducing costs or sheer necessity.

Question 10 Note: Although factors b), c) and d) are significant in making a choice of channel, once that choice is made it is how you use your relative strengths and weaknesses, vis-à-vis your competitors, that will be the springboard to success. Answer = a).

11

Information and organization

In outline, the marketing planning process is simple,
consisting of: a situation review; assumptions; objectives; strategies; programmes; and measurement
and review. The reality, of course, is much more
complex due to the number of contextual issues that
have to be considered, the nature of which will be
unique to each business situation. 'When to plan',
'how often' and 'by whom' are just a few of the questions requiring answers, indicating a much wider
array of practical concerns. Before tackling such
questions (as we will do in the next chapter), it is
important to recognize at the outset that the implementation of a marketing planning system is gov-
erned by two major constraints: information and
organization.

To make marketing planning work, you need
information, so that you can forecast the market, so

**To make marketing
planning work you need
information**

that you can organize your business to cope – and, ideally, to excel. Any marketing plan is only as good as the information on which it is based, and this is why the ongoing collection, storage, analysis and exploitation of meaningful market information is so central to marketing activity. The other key point is that marketing planning occurs within a 'living' environment, that is to say, it affects and is affected by the nuances of company structure and culture. For instance, featuring among the many marketing planning issues is whether or not the company's management style can adapt sufficiently to enable the marketing planning process to deliver the rewards it promises.

INFORMATION

The supply of information presents its own challenges, in terms of having too much or too little, too early or too late, or indeed, of the right kind. The reason why it is so difficult to specify marketing's information needs is that, unlike accounting or manufacturing, which have fixed information needs, marketing's information needs keep changing as the marketing strategy evolves. Further, marketing information has a limited life – it is perishable – so a company's information bank must be constantly replenished.

It is difficult to specify all marketing information needs

A cost/benefit appraisal of all sources of marketing information is required to ensure that investment in such information is justified. One way of estimating how much to spend is based on the theory of probability and expected value. For example, if by launching a product you had to incur development costs of 1 million euros and you estimated there was a 10 per cent chance that the product would fail, the maximum loss expectation would be 100,000 euros (ie, 1 million euros x 0.1). Therefore it is worth spending 10,000 euros to prevent a loss.

Marketing research

As stressed throughout this book, profitable development of the company can only come from a continual commitment to matching the company's capabilities with customers' needs. In order that the company can be certain this matching process is taking place effectively, it is necessary that a two-way information flow exists between the customer and the firm. This is the role of *marketing research*. Marketing research is concerned with the whole marketing process. (Market research is research about markets.)

The difference between marketing research and market research

There are many forms of marketing research to consider, which break down into four basic types:

- Internal – analysis of sales records, advertising levels, price versus volume, etc.

- External – use of sources outside the organization to complement internal research.

- Reactive – responses to questionnaires, structured interviews, etc.

- Non-reactive – interpretation of observed phenomena, eg, filming customers in a store, listening to customer panels, etc.

As there are pros and cons for each type, a mix can be useful. For example, sales records can provide valuable insights, but are not good predictors of future performance as they are restricted to historic performance. Telephone interviews are quick and relatively inexpensive, but limited in the amount of technical information that can be obtained. The starting point of any marketing research programme should be an examination of existing materials, particularly by means of desk research. When combined with internal sales information, the wealth of information available from published information can be the most powerful research method open to a company.

Marketing data, information and intelligence

The gathering of data is only the first step in marketing research. Data must be given direction before it can become relevant information, and information is only relevant if the company has some purpose in mind, some marketing problem to solve. Information allied to purpose becomes *intelligence*: information that is consumable and useable by management in converting uncertainty into measurable risk. Conversion of uncertainty into risk and the minimization of risk is perhaps marketing management's most important task, and marketing research is vital in this process.

Marketing information system (MIS)

A system to facilitate information flows needs to be developed so that there are appropriate inputs and correct data gets to the users in a sensible form. Sound marketing plans rely on sound marketing evidence, and this requires the organization of information into a coherent structure so that planners can match external facts about the market to internal facts and figures. Many companies have turned to technological innovation (eg, database technology) to extract vital information from often unwieldy and complex data.

However, while computerized data collection and analysis can make marketing research easier by automating the reconciliation of internal and external audits, it can also conceal or divert attention from the reality of the situation. Companies are prone to collecting data that is readily available rather than that which is actually needed, and to accumulating data that they do not know how to use. There is also a common assumption that computerized analysis gives definitive results, where in fact, the data used for analysis may be incomplete, out of date, irrelevant, or somehow flawed. Thus the use of information, and the use of IT in managing information, must be guided by good judgement and a well thought through, systematic approach.

Computers are often not the answer

Cranfield's six 'I's model summarizes the ways in which IT generally can add value to the customer and hence improve the organization's marketing effectiveness. It comprises:

- Integration – of data across time and databases.
- Interactivity – beyond addressability to dialogue.
- Individualization – information-enabled tailoring.
- Independence of location – the death of distance.
- Intelligence – informed strategy.
- Industry restructuring – redrawing the market map.

Because all companies are in some ways unique, there are no easy, 'off-the-shelf' marketing information systems. However, there are a few secrets of success in constructing a good one. These are:

- Understanding what marketing needs and particularly how the internal and external views will be reconciled.

- Developing a strong cost-benefit case for information systems, given that other systems, including financial ones, will have to be altered to accommodate the needs of marketing.
- Working continuously with internal IT staff until the system is built. They are under pressure from other sources, especially finance, and unless marketing maintains momentum and direction, then other priorities will inevitably win.

Marketing should take place as close to the customer as possible. Marketing planners must therefore secure cross-functional understanding and cooperation if they are to develop the systems they require to ensure that the company's products meet present and future customer needs. They must build inter-departmental bridges to acquire data, information and knowledge on an ongoing basis.

FORECASTING

As marketing's task continues to increase in size and complexity, the ability to plan ahead effectively is paramount. The growing diversity of customer needs in today's rapidly changing environment has resulted in shorter product life cycles, which have therefore become more difficult to manage profitably. The difficulty of finding and developing profitable markets has made forecasting more hazardous and less accurate still. Before any company can set marketing objectives and strategies it must make some long-range, or macro forecasts of markets in total. Then, when the company has decided what specific market opportunities it wants to take advantage of, it must make detailed unit, or micro forecasts. The type of forecasting will depend upon the: accuracy required; availability of data; time horizon; and position of the product in its life cycle (macro at an early stage).

For maximum accuracy, both macro and micro forecasting require two techniques for forecasting: quantitative and qualitative techniques. Quantitative techniques are based on facts, or statistical probabilities. To account for likely changes to past trends, it is then also necessary to use qualitative methods, such as expert opinions and market research, to predict probable discontinuities.

ORGANIZATION

In addition to issues surrounding marketing information and forecasting, companies also face issues regarding how best to organize for marketing planning. While the marketing planning process itself remains more or less consistent throughout, how that process is managed must be congruent with the current organizational culture. In other words, marketing planning organization must reflect the organizational evolution of the company as it passes through characteristic life phases.

Organizing for marketing planning

As depicted in Figure 11.1, organizational growth is propelled by reaction to crises. At start up the firm is often organized around the owner who tends to know more about customers and products than anyone else in the company (creative evolution). However, as the firm grows in size and complexity, and new products and markets are added, the organizational form breaks down and the owner must either sell up or allocate certain functional duties to specialized departments (directed evolution).

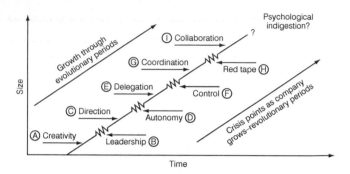

Figure 11.1 Organizational evolution

Eventually these departments seek greater autonomy and a more delegative style of leadership prevails, which generates more autonomy at lower levels (delegated evolution). As growth continues, senior management become seriously concerned about the high levels of autonomy lower down in the organization and try to regain control by establishing better coordination between the various parts of the organization (coordinated evolution). Ultimately, the coordinated practices become institutionalized and thus planning procedures become ritualized, and procedures seem to assume precedence over problem solving. To redress the stifling effects of oppressive bureaucracy or 'red tape', the company strives towards a new phase of collaboration, with greater emphasis on teamwork, creativity and spontaneity (collaborative evolution).

Clearly, each solution to an organizational development problem gives rise to the next evolutionary phase. Since the key to successful marketing is to have a suitable organizational structure, understanding this pattern of structural change can usefully indicate appropriate organizational and planning frameworks. Figure 11.2 tries to encapsulate the

Place an x on each of the four lines below to indicate where your organization lies

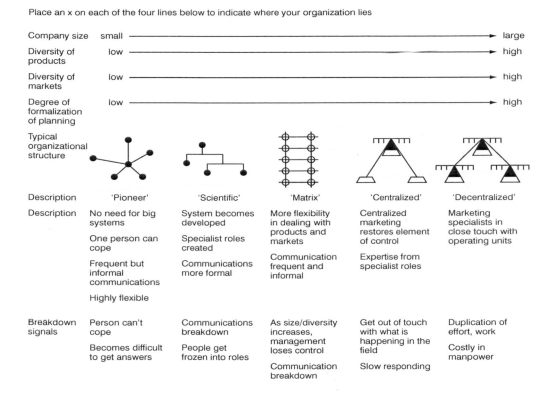

Figure 11.2 Organizational structure

types of organizational structure as they relate to company size and complexity, and the associated degree of formality in the marketing planning process. (To evaluate the appropriateness of your organizational structure, place an x on each of the four lines to indicate where your organization currently lies.)

No one particular organizational form can be recommended, common sense and market needs being the final arbiter. However, the following factors always need to be considered:

• marketing 'centres of gravity';

- interface areas (eg, present / future; salespeople / drawing office; etc);
- authority, responsibility, and accountability;
- ease of communication;
- coordination;
- flexibility;
- human factors.

Organize around customer groups or markets not products, functions or geography

An organization's marketing planning effectiveness is affected significantly by the way that it organizes for marketing. Wherever practicable, it is sensible to organize around customer groups, or markets, rather than around products, functions or geography, so that personnel, accounting, production, distribution and sales policies are tailored to unique sets of market needs. It is also better to put sales and marketing under the supervision of one person so as to ensure proper coordination of these distinct but interrelated functions (see example b) in Figure 11.3). Separation of sales and marketing at board level can cause disparity between what marketing is planning and what sales is doing out in the field. Lack of a suitable

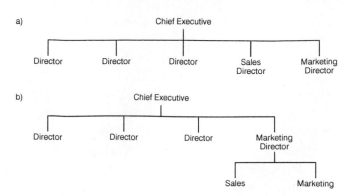

Figure 11.3 Organizing for marketing at board level

organizational structure for an integrated marketing function, compounded by lack of meaningful information about market segments, means that marketing planning is unlikely to be successful.

The main organizational barriers to effective marketing planning can be summarized as:

Barriers to marketing planning

- Cognitive – not knowing enough about marketing planning.
- Cultural – the company culture is not orientated towards marketing planning.
- Political – the culture 'carriers/leaders' feel threatened by marketing.
- Resources – not enough resources are allocated to marketing.
- Structural – lack of a plan and organization for planning.
- Lack of an effective MIS.

To identify what organizational barriers may exist in your firm, so that you can work to overcome them, complete Test 11.1.

Test 11.1: Organizational issues in marketing planning*

You are asked to answer a series of statements about your organization's approach to marketing planning. Since this quest is for useful and genuine data, please try to be as accurate and objective as you can as you complete this document.

You score the questionnaire by entering a number, 1–5, *only in the position indicated by the box next to each statement.* Choose your scores, using these criteria:

1 If you strongly disagree with statement.
2 If you tend to disagree with statement.
3 If you don't know if you agree or disagree.
4 If you tend to agree with statement.
5 If you strongly agree with statement.

A	B	C	D	E

1 The chief executive and directors show an active interest in marketing planning. ☐ (E)

2 The chief executive and directors demonstrate their understanding of marketing planning. ☐ (A)

3 The chief executive and directors use the marketing plan as the basis for making key marketing decisions. ☐ (D)

4 The chief executive and directors allocate adequate resources to ensure the marketing plan is completed satisfactorily. ☐ (B)

5 The need for a marketing plan is clearly explained to all managers. ☐ (A)

6 There is adequate information/data upon which to base a marketing plan. ☐ (B)

7 Our marketing plan has a good balance between short-term and long-term objectives. ☐ (C)

8 People are clear about their role in the marketing planning process. ☐ (E)

---

* This test is taken from *Marketing Plans: How to prepare them; how to use them*, Malcolm McDonald, Butterworth Heinemann, Oxford, 6th Edition, 2007.

	A	B	C	D	E
9 Line managers are trained to understand how the marketing planning process operates.	☐				
10 Line operational managers believe the marketing plan is a useful document.				☐	
11 Enough time is allowed for the planning process.		☐			
12 It is made easy for line managers to understand the plan.	☐				
13 Marketing planning is never starved for lack of resources.		☐			
14 It is reasonable for a company like ours to have a well-thought-out marketing plan.				☐	
15 Reasons for past successes or failures are analysed.			☐		
16 In our organization we don't leave planning just to the planners; other managers have a valuable contribution to make.					☐
17 Our organizational style encourages a sound marketing planning process.				☐	
18 There is clear understanding of the marketing terminology we use in our organization.	☐				
19 Market opportunities are highlighted by the planning process.			☐		
20 Functional specialists contribute to the marketing planning process.					☐
21 We limit our activities so that we are not faced with trying to do too many things at one time.		☐			
22 Taking part in marketing planning in our organization holds a high prospect of being rewarded, either financially or in career terms.				☐	

	A	B	C	D	E
23 Only essential data appear in our plans.			☐		
24 Marketing does not operate in an 'ivory tower'.				☐	
25 From the wealth of information available to use, we are good at picking out the key issues.	☐				
26 There is a balance between narrative explanation and numerical data in our plans.			☐		
27 Our field sales force operates in a way which is supportive to our marketing plan.					☐
28 Our plan demonstrates a high level of awareness of the 'macro' issues facing us.	☐				
29 Inputs to the planning process are on the whole as accurate as we can make them.		☐			
30 Marketing planning is always tackled in a meaningful and serious way.			☐		
31 Our plan doesn't duck the major problems and opportunities faced by the organization.				☐	
32 There is a high awareness of 'micro' issues in our plan.	☐				
33 Our plans recognize that in the short term we have to match our current capabilities to the market opportunites.		☐			
34 Inputs to the marketing planning process are an integral part of the job of all line managers.					☐
35 Marketing planning is a priority issue in our organization.			☐		
36 Our planning inputs are not 'massaged' to satisfy senior executives.		☐			

	A	B	C	D	E
37 People understand and are reasonably happy that our marketing planning process is logical and appropriate.	☐				
38 We use the same time-scale for our marketing plans as we do for finance, distribution, production and personnel.		☐			
39 We view our operational plan as the first year of our long-term plan, not as a separate entity.			☐		
40 Senior executives do not see themselves as operating beyond the confines of the marketing plan.				☐	
41 The advocates of 'correct' marketing planning are senior enough in the company to make sure it happens.			☐		
42 People are always given clear instuctions about the nature of their expected contribution to the marketing plan.		☐			
43 We try to make data collection and retrieval as simple as possible.	☐				
44 Our marketing plans do not go into great detail, but usually give enough information to make any necessary point.			☐		
45 The role of specialists is made quite clear in our planning process.					☐
46 We are always prepared to learn any new techniques that will make our marketing planning process more effective.	☐				
47 The role of marketing planning is clearly understood in the organization.					☐
48 Marketing research studies (by internal staff or agencies) are often used as inputs to our marketing planning process.		☐			

	A	B	C	D	E
49 Our marketing planning is regularly evaluated in an attempt to improve the process.			☐		
50 The chief executive and directors receive information which enables them to assess whether or not the marketing plan is coming to fruition as expected.					☐
TOTAL SCORES					

Add up the total scores in each column.

Interpretation of Test 11.1

Add up the scores for columns **A**, **B**, **C**, **D** and **E** and write them in the boxes provided. Each of the letters represents a potential barrier to marketing planning, namely:

A = Cognitive barrier, ie knowledge and skills.
B = Resource barrier, ie lack of time, people, data.
C = Systems/routine barrier, ie lack of procedures.
D = Organizational climate barrier, ie belief and interest in marketing planning.
E = Behaviour barrier, ie the roles people play

The maximum score for each of these areas is 50 points. The higher the score, the less that potential barrier to marketing is likely to be making an impact. In other words, the areas with low scores (below 30) will probably be the areas worth investigating initially in the search for improvement.

Personal notes

List what actions need to be taken.

QUESTIONS AND ANSWERS

Questions

1. Which of the following is not an example of marketing research?
   a) Research about the effect of pricing on demand.
   b) Research about trends in a specific market.
   c) Research about customer response to advertising.
   d) Research about customer expectations of service.

2. Below are listed some examples of market research methods. Identify which of these are reactive forms of research (R) and which are non-reactive (N).
   a) telephone surveys ( )
   b) consumer observation ( )
   c) user tests ( )
   d) retail audits ( )
   e) using government statistics ( )
   f) pilot testing ( )

3. In general, what is the main danger of basing marketing decisions solely on internal sources of information?
   a) They will not be very accurate.
   b) They will not be in an immediately usable form.
   c) They will contain only historic information.
   d) They will not reflect the total market.

4. Analysis of internal data can usually uncover some useful marketing information. Typically, which of the following would you expect to be able to find from internal sources?
    a) Value of goods sold per customer.
    b) Buyer's name and position.
    c) Reasons for purchase decision.
    d) Volume of goods sold by geographical region.
    e) The competitiveness of your customer package.
    f) Information about customers' buying processes.

5. The Cranfield six 'I's model illustrates ways in which IT can add value to customers. Below are just four of its components, please write the missing ones in the spaces provided.

    integration   independence   ....
                        of location
    industry   individualization   ....
    restructuring

6. In order to set marketing objectives and strategies, which of the following methods of forecasting would be your choice?
    a) Macro forecasting.   b) Micro forecasting.

7. Here is a representation of how organizations experience periods of evolutionary growth as they increase in size and become more mature. Each growth phase gives rise to a phase of turbulence, or crisis, which has to be resolved before it can once again make progress. Please identify (i) the missing growth phase, and (ii) the most appropriate style of marketing planning for that phase.

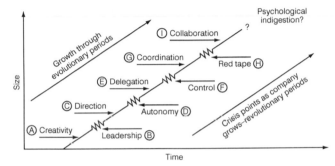

i) ....

ii) The planning approach ought to be:
   a) Bottom up.
   b) Top down.
   c) A mixture of both.

8. Wherever practicable is it best to organize around:
   a) Customer groups.
   b) Product groups.
   c) Geographical areas.
   d) Cost centres.

9. Tick which of the following are typically characteristics of a centralized organizational structure.
   a) There is an unnecessary duplication of tasks and functions.
   b) Decision makers have less feel for the market.
   c) Control tends towards bureaucracy.

d) All units pursue a coordinated marketing strategy.
e) There is great flexibility.
f) There is a high level of synergistic working and creativity.

10. Why is it so difficult to specify marketing information needs?
a) Because IT programmes cannot deliver the right information.
b) Because marketing strategy is constantly evolving.
c) Because organizations are slow to recognize their information requirements.
d) Because accounting information takes priority.

Answers

Question 1   Answer = b). This is an example of market research as opposed to marketing research.

Question 2   Answer: reactive (target audience respond to questions or stimuli) = a) c) and f).
Non-reactive (target audience behaviour is implied by analysing data) = b), d) and e).

Question 3   Answer = c) sales records, etc by their very nature are historic documents and may not be good predictors for the future; and d) unless of course the company has a monopoly and even that does not always guarantee 100 per cent coverage of a market.

Question 4   Answer = a), b) and d).

Question 5   Answer: intelligence and interactivity.

Question 6   Answer = a). It is important to get the 'big picture' first.

Question 7   Answer = i) Direction. ii) = b).

Question 8   Answer = a). These provide the most accurate indicators of what needs have to be met.

Question 9   Answer = b), c) and d). These are common characteristics of a centralized organization.

Question 10 Answer = b). This requires new types of information rather than the fixed and routine.

Note: a). This is a problem of delivering information, not about specifying it. The real problem here lies in the calibre of the management and a lack of proactivity, not the difficulty about specifying information. This may be true, but it is a red herring behind which incompetent managers may hide. The required marketing information should be specified and made an issue in order to get adequate resources.

12

Making marketing planning work

As we have seen in the previous chapter, the required degree of formalization of marketing planning will depend on the company's size and the diversity of its products/markets. As companies get larger, their operational problems get more complex. Written procedures are needed to make the marketing strategy explicit and the marketing concept understood. Thus, the bigger and more diversified the organization, the bigger the need for standardized, formalized procedures.

However, while the degree of formalization will change with organizational evolution, the need for a complete marketing system does not. The problems that companies suffer, then, are a function of either the degree to which they have a requisite marketing planning system or the degree to which the formalization of their system grows with the situational

As organizations grow so does the need for formalized procedures complexities attendant upon the size and diversity of operations. Figure 12.1 explores four key outcomes that marketing planning can evoke.

It can be seen that systems I, III, and IV, ie, where the individual is totally subordinate to a formalized system, or where individuals are allowed to do what they want without any system, or where there is neither system nor creativity, are less successful than system II, in which the individual is allowed to be entrepreneurial within a total system. System II, then, will be an effective marketing planning system,

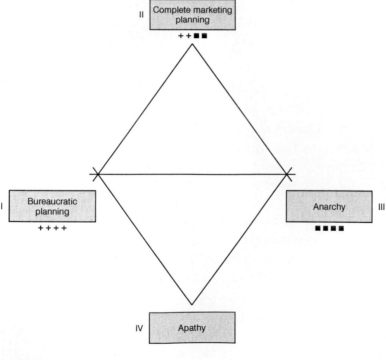

+ Degree of formalization
■ Degree of openness

Figure 12.1 Four key outcomes of marketing planning

but one in which the degree of formalization will be a function of company size and diversity.

The really important issue in any system is the extent to which it enables control to be exercised over the key determinants of success and failure. Research has shown that certain conditions must be satisfied for a marketing planning system to work. There must be:

- Openness. Any closed-loop planning system, especially if it is based just on forecasting and budgeting, will deaden any creative response and will eventually lead to failure. Therefore there has to be some mechanism for preventing inertia from settling in through the over-bureaucratization of the system.

- Integration. Marketing planning that is not integrated with other functional areas of the business at general management level will be largely ineffective.

- Coherence. Separation of operational and strategic marketing planning will lead to a divergence of the short-term thrust of a business at the operational level from the long-term objectives of the enterprise as a whole, with the short-term viewpoint winning because it achieves quick results.

- Leadership. Unless the chief executive understands and takes an active role in strategic marketing planning, it will never be an effective system.

- Time. It can take three years to introduce marketing planning successfully.

As we have seen, a successful marketing planning system follows requisite, key steps:

- There will have to be guidance provided by the corporate objectives.

- A marketing audit must take place.
- A gap analysis must be completed.
- SWOT analyses must be drawn up.
- Assumptions and contingencies must be considered.
- Marketing objectives and strategies must be set.
- Individual marketing programmes must be established.
- There must be a period of measurement and review.

All this work will take time, and will certainly require discussions with other functional departments, either to get information or to ensure collaboration. Thus it is important to schedule the tasks and timing, and to present it in a clear manner, for example, diagrammatically as shown in Figure 12.2. The circle represents a calendar year and the time periods are given as examples to indicate the sequence of planning activities. As the company gets more experienced in planning, then the timetable can probably be tightened up and the whole planning period shortened. In the second planning year, months 11 and 12 could be used to evaluate the first year's plan and thereby prepare information for the next round of corporate planning. The planning process is an iterative one and a continual undercurrent throughout the year.

It is also clear from the planning cycle that key account planning must take place at the same time as, or even before, draft plans are prepared for a strategic business unit.

Significantly, there are two open loop points. These are the key times, or opportunities in the planning

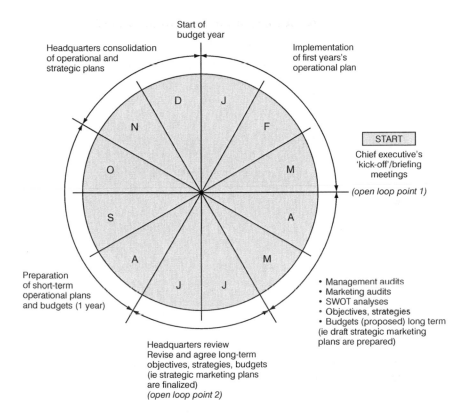

Figure 12.2 Strategic and operational planning – timing

process when a subordinate's views and findings should be subjected to the closest examination by a superior. By utilizing these 'oxygen valves', life can be breathed into marketing planning, transforming it into the critical and creative process it is supposed to be, rather than the dull, repetitive ritual it so often turns out to be.

There is a natural point of focus in the future beyond which it is pointless to plan for. Generally, small firms can use shorter horizons because they tend to be flexible in the way in which they can react to environmental turbulence in the short term. Larger firms need longer lead times in which to make changes in direction and thus require longer planning horizons. While three and five year periods are commonly used, the planning horizon should reflect the nature of the markets in which the company operates and the time needed to recover capital investment costs.

Remaining sensitive and responsive to the marketplace raises another question: Who should make marketing decisions? Top management who are remote from the scene, or those at 'the sharp end' who have intimate knowledge of the markets but less corporate authority? Location of marketing planning within the company is an important aspect of successful marketing planning. Marketing planning should take place as close to the marketplace as possible in the first instance, but the plans should then be reviewed at high levels within the organization to see what issues have been overlooked. One means of formulating an informed, overall strategic view is to conduct a hierarchy of audits and SWOTs at each main organizational level (ie, individual manager, group manager, profit centre, head office) and then to consolidate them.

Since, in anything but the smallest of undiversified companies, it is not possible for headquarters to set detailed objectives for operating units, it is suggested that at the situation review stage of the planning process, strategic guidelines be issued outlining possible areas for which objectives and strategies will be set (eg, financial, operational, human, organizational, marketing), or the chief executive gives a personal briefing at kick-off meetings. Strategic and operational planning must be a

Who should make marketing decisions?

top down and bottom up process. Understanding this total interdependence between upper and lower levels of management in respect of audits and objective and strategy setting is crucial to achieving the necessary balance between control and creativity.

The vital role that the chief executive and top management *must* play in marketing planning underlines a key point. That is, it is *people* who make systems work, and that the system design and implementation have to take account of the 'personality' of both the organization and the people involved, and that these are different in all organizations. The attitudes of executives vary, ranging from the extremes of the impersonal, autocratic kind to the highly personal, participative kind. There is some evidence to indicate that chief executives who fail, firstly, to understand the essential role of marketing in generating profitable revenue in a business, and, secondly, to understand how marketing can be integrated into other functional areas of the business through marketing planning procedures, are a key contributory factor in poor economic performance.

It is people that make systems work

The most common design and implementation problems with marketing planning systems are:

- weak support from the chief executive and top management;
- lack of a plan for planning;
- lack of line management support (hostility; lack of skills/information/resources; inadequate organizational structure);
- confusion over planning terms;
- numbers in lieu of written objectives and strategies;

- too much detail, too far ahead;
- once-a-year ritual;
- separation of operational planning from strategic planning;
- failure to integrate marketing planning into total corporate planning system;
- delegation of planning to a planner.

By contrast, a company with an effective marketing planning system is likely to have:

- widely understood objectives;
- highly motivated employees;
- high levels of actionable market information;
- greater interfunctional coordination;
- minimum wastage of resources;
- acceptance of the need for continuous change and a clear understanding of priorities;
- greater control over the business and less vulnerability from the unexpected.

10 principles of marketing planning

To summarize, then, the 10 principles of marketing planning follow.

1. Develop the strategic plan first; the operational plan is derived from this.
2. Put marketing as close as possible to the customer, and have marketing and sales under one person.
3. Marketing is an attitude of mind, not a set of procedures.
4. Organize activities around customer groups, not functional activities.
5. A marketing audit must be rigorous. No vague terms should be allowed, and nothing should be

hidden. Managers should use tools like portfolio analysis and product life cycle information.

6. SWOT analyses should be focused on segments that are critical to the business; concentrate only on key factors that lead to objectives.

7. People must be educated about the planning process.

8. There has to be a plan for planning.

9. All objectives should be prioritized in terms of their urgency and impact.

10. Marketing planning needs the active support of the chief executive and must be appropriate for the culture of the organization.

As a final exercise in exploring why your marketing plans are not working, or are not working as well as you would wish them to, complete Test 12.1.

Test 12.1: Evaluation of marketing strategy

(Test devised by Brian Smith, CEO Pragmedic – pragmedic@aol.com – as part of his PhD study into marketing planning effectiveness. Used with his kind permission. Copyright remains with Brian Smith.)

Instructions

With your company in mind, tick one answer to each of the following questions.

1. Our marketing strategy makes it clear what markets or parts of the market we will concentrate our efforts on.
    – If your strategy attacks all of your market sector (eg, retail groceries, super-conducting magnets) equally = 0
    – If your strategy is focused by 'descriptor group' (eg, ABC1s, large firms, SMEs, etc.) = 1
    – If your strategy attacks needs-based segments (eg, efficacy focused customers with high ego needs) = 2
    – If you don't know = -1

2. Our marketing strategy makes clear what actions fit with the marketing strategy and what does not.
    – If your strategy allows complete freedom of action = 0
    – If your strategy allows a high degree of freedom of action = 1
    – If your strategy makes the most of your action plan decisions for you = 2
    – If you don't know = -1

3. Our marketing strategy clearly defines our intended competitive advantage in the marketplace.
    – If there is no strong and supported reason why the customer should choose you = 0
    – If there is a reason the customer should buy from you but no strong proof = 1
    – If you can state clearly the reason the customer should buy from you and not the competitor, and substantiate that reason = 2
    – If you don't know = -1

4. Our marketing strategy allows synergy between the activities of the different parts of the organization.
    – If the strategy is a compromise of what each department is capable of = 0
    If the strategy uses the strengths of only one or two departments = 1

- If the strategy uses the best strengths of all departments
  = 2
- If you don't know = -1

5. Our marketing strategy is significantly different from that of our competitors.
  - If you target the same customers with the same value proposition = 0
  - If you target the same customers OR use the same value proposition = 1
  - If you target different customers with a different value proposition = 2
  - If you target different customers with a different value proposition = 2
  - If you don't know = -1

6. Our marketing strategy recognizes and makes full allowance for the needs and wants of our target customers.
  - If you only meet the basic functional needs (safety, regulation, efficacy) = 0
  - If you also meet the higher functional needs (efficiency, service, price) = 1
  - If you also meet the emotional and ego needs (brand, confidence) = 2
  - If you don't know = -1

7. Our marketing strategy recognizes and makes full allowance for the strategies of our competitors.
  - If you are ignoring the competitors' strategies = 0
  - If you are allowing for some of the competitors' strategies = 1
  - If you are allowing for all of the competitors' strategies = 2
  - If you don't know = -1

8. Our marketing strategy recognizes and makes full allowance for changes in the business environment that are beyond our control, such as technological, legislation or social change.
  - If your strategy is designed for today's conditions = 1
  - If your strategy allows for one or two changes (eg, technology or demographics) = 1
  - If your strategy considers the combined effects of all the external factors = 2
  - If you don't know = -1

9. Our marketing either avoids or compensates for those areas where we are relatively weak compared to the competition.
    − If you have taken little or no account of your relative weaknesses = 0
    − If you are trying to fix your relative weaknesses = 1
    − If your strategy means that your relative weaknesses don't matter = 2
    − If you don't know = -1

10. Our marketing strategy makes full use of those areas where we are relatively strong compared to the competition.
    − If you have taken little or no account of your relative strengths = 0
    − If you are trying to use your relative strengths = 1
    − If your strategy means that your relative strengths become more important = 2
    − If you don't know = -1

11. Our marketing strategy, if successfully implemented, will meet all the objectives of the organization.
    − If your strategy, fully and successfully implemented, does not deliver your financial or non-financial objectives = 0
    − If your strategy, fully and successfully implemented, delivers only your financial objectives = 1
    − If your strategy, fully and successfully implemented, delivers your financial and non-financial objectives = 2
    − If you don't know = -1

12. The resources available to the organization are sufficient to implement the marketing strategy successfully.
    − If you have neither the tangible nor the intangible resources to implement the strategy = 0
    − If you have only the tangible or the intangible resource, but not both = 1
    − If you have both the tangible and the intangible resources needed to implement the strategy = 2
    − If you don't know = -1

Scoring and interpretation for Test 12.1

Now add up the scores relating to your 12 answers for a total score. The maximum score for the exercise is 24. If you scored:

18–24	Well done! (Are you sure?)	– Can I buy some shares?
12–17	You will succeed	– If your competition is weak!
6–11	You will survive	– If your competition is weak!
Less than 6		– Oh dear, it was nice knowing you.

QUESTIONS AND ANSWERS

Questions

1. Which of the following statements about marketing planning are true (T) or false (F)?
    a) Any closed-loop marketing planning system based on forecasts and budgets leads to a creative marketing response. (   )
    b) The separation of responsibility for operational and strategic marketing planning leads to a preoccupation with short-term results. (   )
    c) Planning undertaken by the marketing function will be successful as long as inter-departmental politics do not lessen its impact. (   )
    d) Marketing planning will never be effective unless the chief executive gives it his/her blessing and involvement. (   )

2. To a large extent the degree of formality of the marketing planning system can be related to company size and market or product diversity. The matrix below shows the possible combinations of

these factors. Please match quadrants A, B, C and D with the appropriate descriptions of formality a, b or c given below.

Company size

	Large	Small
Wide	A	B
Product or market diversity	C	D
Narrow		

Quad A   ( )   Quad C   ( )
Quad B   ( )   Quad D   ( )

a) Low degree of formalization.
b) Medium degree of formalization.
c) High degree of formalization.

3. Which of the factors below contribute to the low level of marketing planning formality in a small company? Mark true (T) or false (F).
a) Top managers have an in depth knowledge of products and customers. ( )
b) Formality is not the culture of most small companies   ( )
c) There are few top managers and they work in close proximity of each other. ( )
d) The range of products or services is usually not complicated.   ( )

4. Complete the following sentence with the most
    accurate ending of those listed below.

    The really important issue in any marketing
    planning system is the degree to which:
    a) it enables control to be exercised over the key
        determinants of success and failure;
    b) it is compatible with all the other company
        planning procedures;
    c) it can be understood by the management and
        staff;
    d) it clarifies the roles of those who figure in the
        marketing plan.

5. Many companies claim that their marketing plan-
    ning will enable them to achieve the following
    goals: to increase sales; to maximize profits; to
    increase market share; and to minimize operating
    costs. Is this belief realistic, or an impossibility?
    a) realistic   b) impossible

6. Another way of looking at the way companies
    implement marketing planning is to consider
    the degree to which their concern for planning
    matches their concern for involving those who
    have a contribution to make to the plan. Again
    these two factors can be combined in the follow-
    ing matrix.

    Your task is to match the matrix quadrants
    A–D with the descriptive labels a–d.

Concern for planning

Low   High

High A	B
Concern for staff involvement	
C	D
Low	

a) anarchic planning   ( )
b) apathetic planning   ( )
c) bureaucratic planning   ( )
d) integrated planning   ( )

7. Here are some definitions about the purpose of marketing planning. Which are true (T) and which are false (F)?

a) To create a sustainable advantage. ( )
b) To integrate the organization's functions profitably. ( )
c) To create profitable customer demand. ( )
d) To match intelligently our capabilities with customer needs. ( )
e) To be the best performing company in the business. ( )

8. The role of the chief executive in the marketing planning process is generally agreed to be which of the following?

a) To define the organizational framework.
b) To act as a catalyst in obtaining inputs from all divisions or departments.

c) To monitor the agreed plans.
d) To maintain the balance between short and
    long-term objectives.
e) To provide a momentum for the planning
    process.
f) To provide the planning structure and systems.

9. What ought to be the strategic planning horizon
    for a company's marketing plan?
    Should it be:
    a) 1 year?   c) 5 years?
    b) 3 years?   d) It depends on the
                           circumstances?

10. There are some basic underlying principles
    about marketing planning. Which of those listed
    below are true (T) or false (F)?
    a) The strategic and operational plans
        can be developed concurrently.   (   )
    b) Marketing is an attitude of mind as
        well as a process.   (   )
    c) Don't get too close to customers because
        emotions will take over from logic.   (   )
    d) A thorough SWOT analysis should be
        conducted on every market segment.   (   )
    e) Objectives should be prioritized in
        terms of their impact.   (   )
    f) A plan for planning evolves as the
        plan develops.   (   )

Answers

Question 1   Answer: a) = F, b) = T, c) = F, d) = T

Question 2   Answer:
A = c). A large company with a diverse range of products or markets needs formal planning procedures to ensure that the complex data is handled in a predetermined and consistent way.
B = b). Although the company is small, a reasonable amount of formality is required to enable it to deal with its diverse operations.
C = b). A degree of formalization is required because of the company size.
D = a). A very simple and informal approach would suit this situation.

Question 3   Answer: all are true, which makes it relatively easy to plan without having to resort to a complicated planning procedure.

Question 4   Although b), c) and d) are clearly beneficial features of any planning system, it is gaining control over the key determinants of success and failure that is really important. Thus the answer is a).

Question 5   Answer = b). The stated objectives are not mutually supportive, for example, to gain market share may require prices to be low, which is in conflict with maximizing profits. Similarly, increasing sales may require an investment in advertising or more sales staff, which increases rather than minimizes operating costs.

Question 6   Answer:
a) = A. With a low concern for planning and with everyone getting involved, no doubt with each person pursuing their vested interests, anarchy will rule.
b) = C. Here the low concern about anything constructive will result in apathy.
c) = D. Here the concern for planning takes precedent over peoples' contributions. When this happens it is not unusual to find sterile, bureaucratic planning procedures.
d) = B. Clearly the two concerns are not mutually exclusive. This quadrant integrates the two to best effect.

Question 7   Answer: T = a) and d). F = b), c) and e). It is only by first matching the capabilities to customer needs and creating a sustainable competitive advantage that these conditions will arise.

Question 8   Answer = a), d) and e). It is the role of the CEO to create the conditions where marketing planning can take place. He or she does not necessarily have to chase around to ensure that everyone is doing their job.

Question 9   Answer = d). While 3 and 5 years are popular choices, the planning horizon needs to reflect the nature of the product and the time necessary to recover capital investment costs resulting from the introduction of new strategies.

Question 10 Answer: T = b) and e). F = a) the operational plan can only be developed after the longer-term strategic goals have been established, c) it is important to get as close to customers as possible, d) it will not be necessary to carry out a thorough SWOT unless segments are important, and f) a plan for planning must be agreed at the outset.

13

Next steps...

The purpose of this short section is to help you consider what activities might be ahead of you as you proceed with the preparation of your marketing plans.

THE MARKETING PLAN
PERFORMANCE MAP®

The Marketing Plan *Performance Map®* is a rigorous diagnostic tool (software supported) that will help you to identify the key areas for you to work on, and to evaluate your progress. It will also help to highlight where your problems lie, giving you a chance to do something about them before they become insurmountable. Details of this tool can be got from INSIGHT, as shown overleaf.

TRAINING AND CONSULTANCY

INSIGHT Marketing and People is able to provide both training and consultancy on helping you to develop you marketing plans, including the use of the EXMAR software, designed to help automate many elements of the planning process. INSIGHT specializes in company work, but does also run a Marketing Planning *Masterclass*. Details of this event can be got by contacting INSIGHT as shown below:

INSIGHT Marketing and People
1 Lidstone Court
Uxbridge Road
George Green
Slough
SL3 6AG
United Kingdom

tel: +44 (0) 1753 822 990
fax: +44 (0) 1753 822 992
e-mail: customer.service@insight-mp.com
 Peter.Cheverton@insight-mp.com
web site: www.insight-mp.com

FURTHER READING

Cheverton, P (2004) *Key Marketing Skills: A complete action kit of strategies, tools and techniques for marketing success*, Kogan Page, London

Cheverton, P (2003) *Key Account Management: A complete action kit of tools and techniques for achieving profitable key supplier status*, 3rd edn, Kogan Page, London

McDonald, M (2007) *Marketing Plans: How to prepare them; how to use them*, 6th edn, Butterworth-Heinemann, London

Index